A Practical Guide to Happiness

How to Bring Optimism, Confidence, and Self- Worth into Your Life

Max G. Ansbacher

Elizaville Press

Dedication

This book is dedicated with love

in memory of my parents:

Heinz and Rowena Ansbacher

Contents

Dedication iv

Acknowledgments vii

Preface viii

Chapter 1: How "Get Real/Think Positive"Improved My Personal Life..1

Chapter 2: How "Get Real/Think Positive" Improved My Career 11

Chapter 3: The Three Great Rules 29

Chapter 4: What Is Happiness? 49

Chapter 5: The Difference Between Pleasure and True Happiness ...58

Chapter 6: Thirteen Ways to Lift Your Spirits....................................67

Chapter 7: Do Something by Yourself and for Yourself.......................80

Chapter 8: How to Bring Peopleinto Your Life 110

Chapter 9: Preconditions That Block Your Happiness 135

Chapter 10: Behavior Patterns That Rob You of Happiness.............145

Chapter 11: Getting Serious AboutYour Life 178

Chapter 12: Other People...186

Chapter 13: How Mental Health Professionals Can Help 195

Closing Thoughts...208

Postlude 210

Acknowledgments

It gives me great pleasure to acknowledge the significant contributions that my wife Christine has made to the completion of this book by both her writing and editing and by taking such good care of me during the writing process.

I also acknowledge the expert editorial assistance given to me by my brother Ben, the great encouragement given to me by my wonderful PT instructor Kristin Kramer; the help given to me by my friend and fellow author Lynn Gillis; the assistance of Enid Klass; and the competency of Keisha Jerry, Vice President of Ansbacher Investment Management, who made it possible for me to devote so much of my time to this book.

I must also express my gratitude to my brilliant computer advisors, Jack Casais, in New York and Jeff Spiers in Palm Beach, without whom this book could not have been produced.

And finally, I wish to thank all the many people, named and unnamed, who gave me ideas, examples, true life stories, quotes, and family histories which added immeasurably to this book.

Preface

This book turns traditional roads to happiness upside down by advising that instead of working almost to exhaustion to get what you want, you can learn to want what you already have. You have the wonderful pleasure that your friends give you, you have your health, and you have enough money so that you never need to go hungry. The list of good things you already have can go on and on. Following this rule can lead you directly to a more joyful life because it encourages you to realize how lucky you are to have so much!

This rule is just one of the three basic pillars of happiness, which are described in the first part of the book. The remainder is filled with practical tips on how you can execute these rules in specific situations, such as how to make a phone call you are dreading; how to make more friends; how to avoid feeling self-pity or guilt, and relieve the anger from serious events like divorce, death of a loved one, bankruptcy, or a diagnosis of a life-threatening disease, and what you can do when there is nothing specifically wrong, but you just don't seem to enjoy life anymore the way you used to.

In short, this is a book with a solid foundation expressed in my three golden rules, which are followed up with countless detailed examples showing you exactly how to apply them to situations that you may encounter in your everyday life. Taken as a whole, these exercises and action-oriented steps will noticeably raise your feelings of self-esteem, confidence, gratitude, and optimism, making you a happier person.

Chapter 1: How "Get Real/Think Positive" Improved My Personal Life

"Happiness is a direction, not a place."

– Sydney J. Harris, American Journalist (1917 – 1986)

"Why me?" I wondered, staring blankly in the air.

"Why can't I be in the top 1%?"

"Why am I lagging behind?"

"Why did my relationship end?"

My mind flooded me with lots of whys after whys.

I have asked such questions to myself on many occasions, strongly believing that I'm UNhappy.

Ironically, I'm HAPPY that I asked those questions and raised those doubts.

Well, what do you think the most important thing is to motivate you to become be happy?

It is being unhappy. Of course, that is!

Now, don't get me wrong. What I really mean to say is that we must realize the emotions we're going through.

If you don't know you're lost, how will you find your way?

Happiness is a state of mind for the satisfaction of needs or the achievement of goals. We try to chase it and find the magic formula to eternal happiness. However, it differs and is measured from psychological, sociological, economic, and even genetic viewpoints. On the whole, happiness means different things for different people, i.e., it can mean money, fame, a successful career, good education, relationships, goal achievement and charity among others. As I have found it, I can say that happiness doesn't depend on how much we have or how much more we can have. It's about what we have NOW and how it works for us. And it led me to a wonderful discovery—the "Get Real/Think Positive" approach.

For most of my life, I have been plagued by unhappiness, which was brought about by what seemed at the time to be compelling reasons for me to be unhappy.

I suffered through a series of events from college and into my 70s that caused me to feel not just sad or blue but depressed and miserable too. I came to believe I was a failure in many areas of my life and deserved to be unhappy.

Everybody wants to be happy. However, many people feel that they don't deserve it and that there's something wrong with them that makes them unworthy of happiness. In reality, it isn't a question of deserving to be happy, but it's about accepting that we already deserve it.

I realize that all these thoughts were expressions of my feeling of low self-esteem and lack of optimism. My "ah-ha" moment came when I recognized that holding onto these self-critical and debilitating thoughts contributed nothing toward solving my problems. What I needed to do was an objective analysis looking at only the facts surrounding my situation and then drawing conclusions, no matter how bleak they might be. I did this inventory and gave it the handle "Get Real," which simply meant I had to look at the facts of my unfortunate situation in a realistic way and, importantly, without emotion.

Then, next, it was important to "Think Positive." This meant I should examine all aspects of my misfortune to discover if there were any positives that could give me a sense of hope, confidence, and purpose.

I experienced two major problems, or rather two major teachers, that tested me in my personal life. They actually introduced me to the "Get Real/Think Positive" approach, which helped me objectively analyze those problems; in turn, the approach helped me revive my optimism.

The first problem revolved around my academics. I went to an elite private high school called Exeter and got high marks. In college, I was on the Dean's List almost every semester all four years. However, I was still not good enough to even be in the top 20% of my class in law school. And that was hard to swallow. It got even worse when I learned I was just barely in the upper half of my class.

I was studying as hard as I could, but I was, in my opinion, still underperforming. My dream of being a top student who was a member of the prestigious Law Journal evaporated. I felt like a failure, constantly plagued by negative thoughts.

I knew this would also negatively impact my job offers upon graduation. I felt stressed-out, hopeless, and helpless to change my situation, and my self-confidence plummeted – not just in law school but for a few years afterward. I didn't dare think or utter the word "depressed" to myself or my parents. Why? Because both my parents were psychologists.

I hadn't yet developed my strategy of "Get Real/ Think Positive." So, let's look in the rearview mirror together, and with hindsight, let me share with you my objective analysis and how I "Coulda, Shoulda" looked at my misfortune back then.

The "Get Real" Stage

I was attending Yale Law, the school that was usually ranked #1 among all the law schools in the U.S. Naturally, it attracted large numbers of the top law school applicants; most were Phi Beta Kappa or had been in the top 3% of their college class.

Thinking of my situation in this way made me realize why it was going to be so much harder to be in the top half of my law school class compared to my college class. And things started making sense.

I should have realized I had the wrong goal. After all, one had to be very capable to even be admitted to Yale Law. To be unhappy just because I wasn't near the top of my class was totally an <u>unreasonable</u> expectation on my part.

I knew I wasn't a legal genius, so I reasoned I should <u>never</u> have set my expectations at being an "A" student on Law Journal.

How did I turn things around to "Think Positive?"

I realized that because the admission standards at Yale were so high, just being in the middle of my law school class was a wonderful achievement!

Although Yale Law only admitted people who were virtually all in the top 3% of their college classes, regardless of their brilliance, it was mathematically a fact that 97% of the entire law school class could not get into the top 3% of their law school class! In fact, just staying in the school and graduating was a laudable accomplishment.

Looking at my situation from this point of view would have greatly, if not completely, stemmed my feelings of failure. I could have finally told people proudly I graduated from Yale Law.

Now, let's get onto a current example. Not so long ago, I was in my 70s, and a big source of my unhappiness stemmed from my lack of having any children and grandchildren. It got worse when I reflected on how much joy so many people receive from these relationships; I was crestfallen.

Again, applying "Get Real/Think Positive" worked to help me turn around what I thought was a permanent, negative scenario.

When I objectively analyzed the facts to "Get Real," I had to admit that:

I felt a lack of companionship and camaraderie in my life that my wife and friends couldn't fill.

Many of my brothers had grandchildren named after them, and I would have liked my name to live on into the next generation too.

I missed out on sharing two of life's greatest experiences – pregnancy and childbirth and could never recapture them.

However, when I thought of the number of people who never married; the number who never had children; and the number who have children and grandchildren whom they rarely see or talk to, I realized that millions of other people were in my position, and I wasn't being singled out.

Another important fact was that almost everyone I know who's childless isn't unhappy over it. So, why should I pity myself for something that's such a common occurrence?

And then came the "Think Positive." What are the good aspects of my current situation that can make me more optimistic?

Several of my friends have told me they were spending so much time with their grandchildren that it was crowding out other activities they wanted to do. Guess what? That's one problem I've NEVER had.

Other people have told my wife and me that being childless or not having grandchildren can be an unexpected blessing because they have more time and energy for their own pursuits. I found many other things such as:

- We have more freedom to travel.
- Greater career flexibility.

We don't have dependents that we have to make sacrifices for.

There's much less emotional stress in our lives.

We're free from lifelong responsibilities, worries, and potentially serious problems stemming from children and grandchildren.

Lastly, a nephew gave me a beautiful present when he named his son Max. Thus, the tradition in my family of having all my brother's names live on will continue.

Then I started thinking about what I could do to develop alternate relationships with children and young people.

I have seven wonderful nieces and nephews, and most of them have children now. I decided that if I was more involved in their lives, it could be a partial substitute for grandchildren. I do enjoy telephoning them occasionally and seeing them on holidays, which has turned out to be a wonderful and emotionally-satisfying experience.

So, that was the first major problem, and I overcame it all with a practical approach.

The next situation is catastrophic for most people, but not one that I have experienced. One of the most serious blows to anyone's equilibrium is divorce. No matter whether it was you or your spouse who wanted it, whether it was a happy marriage for the most part or not, the emotional damage of divorce is almost always severe and long-lasting.

If this happened to me, I would try to apply the "Get Real/Think Positive" principle to this tragic situation. First, let's evaluate "Get Real." In this situation, you could say to yourself:

- I'll never get married again.
- I don't think I'll be able to lead a happy life when I'm all alone.
- My marriage didn't work out even though so many of my friends are happily married and are such good role models. I guess I'm just not meant to get married.
- I chose an inappropriate person to be my spouse. So, I can't trust my judgment in the future.
- My marriage ended because of infidelity. Now, I can't ever trust anyone again.
- I devoted years of my life to something that didn't work. Now, my looks are fading, and I'm poorer for the experience.

"Think Positive" means, instead of wallowing in self-pity over this calamitous event, you think about divorce in an objective manner and find facts that bring you hope.

- Change doesn't come all at once, and meeting someone I value will take time.
- Most of the people I know who are divorced have moved on with their lives and have restored their equilibrium.

- If many of my divorced friends have found someone whom they wanted to marry, I should be able to do the same.
- Data shows that most people who get divorced do get remarried. So, while this doesn't guarantee that I will, it does shift the odds in my favor.
- I need to fill my life with other activities and people and not wallow in self-pity.
- I'm just a normal person who made a mistake, and everyone makes mistakes in their life.

I've shared two of the biggest disappointments that can cause sadness and years of suffering in anyone's personal life. It's my hope that my "Get Real/Think Positive" system of objectively evaluating misfortunes can lead you to enjoy long-lasting feelings of optimism, confidence, and self-worth.

Chapter 2: How "Get Real/Think Positive" Improved My Career

"Success is not the key to happiness. Happiness is the key to success. If you love what you are doing, you will be successful."

– ***Albert Schweitzer, Austrian Theologian*** (1875 – 1965)

"An employee or an employer: who is happier?"

"A small business owner or the President of a large corporation: who is happier?"

I have seen people debate these and many such questions and have read many studies on such topics.

In your view, who is happier in the above questions or similar questions?

I hope you have chosen your side.

Now, the next questions are:

- Have you ever met unhappy employees?
- Have you ever met unhappy employers?

We all have met unhappy employees and employers, and many of us have been unhappy in either of the statuses. You see, we can find unhappy people everywhere and at every level.

When I was working as a stockbroker, and later when I formed my firm, I couldn't play catch-up with those Wall Street "big boys." And that was enough to make me unhappy. I had a sufficient income stream, but it still couldn't make me happy. Why? Because I started comparing my possessions with what I didn't have. Of course, I never knew for sure if the people who owned those things were really happy.

The point I'm trying to drive home here is that we can't tie happiness to a specific notion, state, or status.

To be honest, happiness is right within you, waiting to be found. Happiness is found by those who seek it with a sincere and practical approach.

In Chapter 1, I shared several personal calamities that brought me to my knees emotionally. In this chapter, I'll be talking about the setbacks that I faced in my professional career. So, let's get on the backward time machine and see a few glimpses of how I got from being a stockbroker to owning a successful company. And most importantly, how I found and applied the formula of finding happiness!

I was a stockbroker at Bear Stearns, and it was a pressure cooker environment. The rule was simple: Produce income for the firm, or you were out.

The first thing I did when I got to my desk at 7:30 am was to see where the market was expected to open, then check if there was any pre-market news on my favorite stocks or if I had gotten any voicemails.

I read long, detailed reports from the research department and checked to see if any of my customers had gotten margin account calls. Then I'd call some of my main clients to discuss the market and the economy. My assistant constantly came by to update me. Then I would start cold calling, my main job for the balance of the day.

That meant that I would call strangers to explain why they should open an account with Bear Stearns and me. The only break in this frenetic activity all day was going for a full American breakfast in the swanky

Executive Dining Room with fellow VP and broker, Jerry Sollen. When the market closed at 4:15 pm, I went home.

While I was at Bear Stearns, I became seriously interested in the new market for Exchange Traded Options, also called listed options, which began in 1973. So, I opened a second account for myself, which would demonstrate how well my new options strategy performed.

After that account had done extremely well for a year, I started using its results in my calls to prospective clients. I also wrote a best-selling book on options in 1983; my book appeared regularly on CNN and Bloomberg, touting my options "Ansbacher Index" as to whether I was bearish or bullish at the moment. After about a year and a half, Bear Stearns learned about this. They called me and told me they were surprised that I didn't know what I was doing was totally illegal!

It turned out that SEC regulations prohibited stock brokers from disclosing their performance records. What a surprise! They reprimanded me, and I immediately had to stop giving out my results to prospects and to clients.

When I thought about what had happened, I realized that those results were basically the only compelling reason I had for obtaining new customers. As long as I worked for any brokerage firm, I wouldn't be able to use them. However, if I left to form my own firm, those results could become the official results of my new firm, and I would be able to promote them.

I realized that if I expected to succeed in my career, I had to leave the Bear. I regretted leaving the many friends I had made there over my 20-year career, especially Daniel Jones, with whom I still have regular lunches 46 years after I met him. Thus, the decision to strike out on my own in 1995 was not an easy one to make.

On my final day, the Chairman of Bear Stearns, Allen "Ace" Greenberg, who was revered by all the employees, called me to his office to wish me good luck on my new venture. He informed me I could keep all my clients who wanted to follow me. I was also fortunate that at that same time, Erin Tower, a friend of mine and fellow broker at Bear, was thinking of leaving. I invited her to join me in my new firm, and soon afterward, I was thrilled to open my own brand-new brokerage firm, Ansbacher Investment Management Inc, with my flagship hedge fund, Elizaville Partners, LLP, specializing in Exchange Traded Options.

I retained most of my clients from Bear and began to attract more by speaking at financial conferences. The best way I was able to grow my business was by using "third-party marketers" who were licensed brokers. Let me tell you here that nothing is unimportant and small in business, especially when you're starting out your venture. These third-party marketers proved to be a great asset for me to grow my business network and opportunities.

I appointed these third-party marketers to represent me to new investors in exchange for paying them 20% of the fees I received on the accounts that they had brought in. One of the most successful third-party marketers was Sal Accardo, an old friend of mine, who eventually brought in nearly half my new customers.

I also appointed a successful third-party marketer, John O'Day, who brought in a prestigious Mitsubishi account from Japan. Yes, I had finally gotten one client in the major league!

One day my colleague, Erin, said to me, "Max, I just met a young man who is a bartender at the Shelburne Hotel. He's desperate to get a job on Wall Street. He's willing to work for nothing. Do you think we could try him out for a while?" Even though she wasn't sure if he had even graduated from high school, and he had no experience in finance, he had a lot of determination. She pointed out that a bartender had to demonstrate the ability to "schmooze" with customers and "sell" them drinks. So, I decided to try him out.

He was really a quick learner and got along well with our clients. So, we started paying him, then gave him a number of pay raises, and eventually even gave him a percentage of our profits. He stayed with us for over fifteen years!

Over time, things started taking off, and we needed more customers for further growth. So, I started speaking at investor conferences two to three times a year, which were designed to introduce investors to managers like me. They usually attracted hundreds of investors and almost as many hedge fund managers. Since my fund was so small compared to the "big boys," it wasn't easy to pick up new customers for my firm. However, I had to try out and utilize what I had to attract more and more investors. So, I sat down and prepared persuasive presentations and messages. In fact, I made the following three-fold message to convince investors at these conferences:

1. My options strategy produced good returns with a partial limit on losses. This loss limit was due to the stop-loss orders we used. Stop-loss orders are instructions to the trading floors to close out a position when it's losing a certain amount of money. They usually work well. But if they're triggered, they become orders to get out of the option at whatever its price is at that time. If the market is crashing, it might not be possible to get out at the price of the stop-loss order, and it would be filled at a worse price. That's why I said we were only partially hedged. I pointed out, however, that it was still far better than not having a stop-loss order at all like some big hedge funds did...and then eventually "exploded."
2. My fund didn't trade individual stocks but only traded the S&P 500 Index, which is composed of 500 stocks, thus offering enormous diversification.
3. Finally, while our results could be similar to the stock market, they were not the same as the stock market, thus offering further diversification to stock investors while remaining invested in the equity area.

This three-fold message brought us many investors and, of course, income. Ultimately, it should have been translated into happiness, lots of happiness. But, for most of my life, I have been plagued by unhappiness, which was brought about by what seemed to me at the time to be extremely compelling reasons.

When I applied this to my career, I used to ask myself why, despite starting my financial career at about the same time as others, do so many guys manage billions of dollars in their hedge funds while I manage only $140 million, much less than one percent of that? I thought if that's not being a failure, then what is? And this situation was my fault. I chose to overlook my $140 million and see the billions that others had.

All these thoughts were expressions of my feeling of low self-esteem and lack of optimism.

But why should I suffer when I should and could actually be happy?

So, I applied the "Get Real" rule to my situation in 1998, three years after starting my firm. I identified the following realities:

First, after analyzing the source of my client base, I realized that there was no way I could ever reasonably expect to have a fund as large as that of the Wall Street "big" boys as they fashioned themselves. Virtually all the founders of big hedge funds started by working for large asset management firms where they could get experience running hedge funds and meet major institutional investors.

When they decided to form their own hedge funds, they simply brought a few of their old customers with them and immediately had hundreds of millions of dollars to start up their new fund. In my case, I had worked only as a stockbroker with individual investors as clients who naturally had much smaller accounts than institutions. Thus, I could never play catch-up with the big boys.

Second, I worked out of a small "bullpen-style" office in a business center that I rented by the month with a lean staff of two. I rented the conference room when I needed to meet with a prospect. This antecedent of We Works was very presentable, but it didn't convey the prestige and success I wanted my firm to convey to prospects.

Third, instead of starting my firm with two seasoned professionals in hedge fund management, I brought with me a stockbroker colleague from Bear Stearns, Erin Towers, and I gave a former bartender a chance to join my business, who loved the stock market and wanted to break into Wall Street in the worst way.

Surprisingly, these three points were all I could think of. And none of the points compares to what the founders of big hedge funds do.

The next step was to "Think Positive." I asked myself what the good things were in this situation. I believed then, as I do now, you should always be able to find something good that results from a bad situation, even a tragedy, if you look hard enough.

As I applied the "Think Positive" rule, I came up with the following points:

- When I calculated the current income from my

fund, I found it was enough to pay my staff and business expenses as well as provide my wife and me with a very comfortable lifestyle.

- Despite my firm's small size, I had already made the first move to attract new investors to my hedge fund by hiring third-party marketers who had brought in a handful of individual investors and one big institution.
- I had already agreed to participate in listing information about our financial results on the platform of a large bank, which could bring us to the attention of many prospects. Thus, my current size might increase.
- Despite my fund not attracting large investors, my performance record of making money for clients was impressive. In 1997, the fund was the top-performing options fund in the US, up 92%, which ought to make it easier to attract prospects.

After my performance record got exposure via the internet, I was invited to speak regularly at investor conferences.

I added more third-party marketers to bring in qualified prospects that became clients, and I took a yearly lease on an entire floor in the tower of a building on Madison Avenue in the 50s with amazing views.

My business grew and prospered over the next decade between 1997 and 2007. Maybe, I would never need to use "Get Real" and "Think Positive" again. But never say never!

> "Behind every success, there's a lot of unsuccessful years."
>
> ***— Bob Brown, Professor, University of St Thomas, MN (1935-2021)***

On September 15, 2008, my hedge fund was hit by an avalanche in the form of the Lehman Brothers bankruptcy. Lehman was not just another stockbroker. It was the fourth-largest firm in the US with assets of over $630 billion and had roots going back to before the Civil War. Its bankruptcy was, and still is, the largest in US history, and it pulled the entire stock market down into the biggest sinkhole since the Great Depression of the 1930s.

My hedge fund suffered along with most of the others, but that didn't help me very much. I take my business seriously, and my level of day-to-day happiness is greatly determined by how well my investment management business is doing. That is why you can imagine how I felt when Lehman Brothers filed for bankruptcy. The panic on Wall Street rained disaster on my hedge fund.

I wondered at one point if I should continue in business after losing so much of my investors' money. It was a difficult decision to make, especially since I was racked with remorse and guilt.

The "Get Real" part meant I had to look at the facts of this bleak situation head-on, accept them as they were, and make a heartbreaking list of what was left after the fallout. I found out the following points:

- My investors suffered huge losses of up to 40%, and over half of them left me. (Since then, I have installed procedures designed to avoid losing that much money in the future.) However, these procedures couldn't undo what had already happened.
- All that remained of my firm were a few investors and friends who had greatly reduced investments.
- My income from the fund was cut to a fraction of what it had been earlier, but my expenses remained almost as high as they were before the disaster.
- I was personally losing thousands of dollars every month to keep the business running.
- The huge losses I was accumulating each month could only be reduced by cutting our expenses significantly. This meant dismissing most of the staff and shifting our business operations to much smaller offices. Would the firm be able to survive such drastic measures?
- As bad as all that was, I also suffered enormous anguish from the belief that I was a complete failure as a money manager.

The next step was to "Think Positive." I asked myself, "what were the good things in this situation?" I believed then, as I do now, you should always be able to find something good that results from a bad situation, even a tragedy, if you look hard enough.

The first fact I discovered was that almost all Wall Street managers had suffered percentage losses comparable to mine. My loss didn't mean that I was an incompetent manager. It only meant that it was a truly terrible stock market that triggered my loss and the loss of almost all other managers on Wall Street.

The second fact was that several other Wall Street big boys "exploded" when they had no stop-loss orders on the floor of the exchange and were forced to shut down. I was still standing, however.

My fund's performance in the immediate six months after the crash was better than many of the big boys. And this was very consoling.

Then another positive aspect dawned on me. My options strategy had always been one that had a large component of risk embedded in it. I mentioned this to every new investor. I spelled it out in excruciating detail in the disclosure document, which every investor is required to read before investing. So, in the wake of a mega stock market fall, my loss should not have been a complete surprise to my investors.

It turned out the financial hit I took was not permanent because I had enough capital to continue trading. If the firm were to make as much money in the future as it had in the past, we could offset the loss in just five or six years. This was a substantial period, but it meant that the current loss was not necessarily the end of my business!

Then I reminded myself that a few years before the financial crash, I had a very small firm with a staff of just two, and we worked out of a small office. I concluded that if it became necessary, I could operate that way once again.

Finally, I embraced the fact that I really enjoyed what I did, that it was challenging, fulfilling, and important to me.

> "Whenever you see a successful business, someone once made a courageous decision."
>
> ***— Peter Drucker, the legendary American business consultant (1909-2006)***

It was my "Think Positive" analysis that gave me the courage with which to answer the question of whether I should stay in business or not. And I did.

My firm, Ansbacher Investment Management, is still in business today and is one of the oldest options trading firms. My fund, Elizaville Partners L.P., began trading almost at the inception of exchange traded options. Over the past 26 years, my strategy has won dozens of awards, including a number of top 10 Options Performance Awards awarded by BarclayHedge, one of the most respected organizations for ranking alternative investment data.

In fact, since 2009, just one year after the crash of 2008, when I was despondent and contemplating closing my firm, I received this award and did so every year with the exception of 2017. Even during the year of COVID (2020), I managed to win it again. So, I've frequently managed to produce superior returns for my clients in all kinds of markets – good and bad.

Whether you're an individual or a business, you can adopt my technique to overcome difficult situations. It's already in use by thousands across the country using different nomenclature. For example, it's the discipline under which first responders operate when they respond to 911 calls that report terrible accidents and emergency health problems.

If you or I came upon an accident where a person's leg had been severed, and blood was gushing, and the person was screaming with pain, we might think, "Oh my God! I don't know what to do, and I can't handle this." But the trained EMT professionals, whether they're police, firefighters, or ambulance personnel, know that panic isn't an option. They stay emotionless and immediately survey the situation to decide what the most important first moves should be to save the victim's life.

You may not have faced such a serious life-threatening situation, but when bad news strikes, your immediate reaction will likely be an emotional one:

- Why did this happen to me?
- How can I be so unlucky?
- It's completely unfair that this happened to me.
- If only I had acted differently, this would never have happened.
- Or worse, "It's all my fault."

All these are expressions of your emotions. While they're valid thoughts, they don't contribute <u>anything</u> to solving your problem.

This is where "Get Real" comes in. It means looking at the facts of the...

accident	double whammy
calamity	meltdown
collapse	misadventure
cataclysm	misfortune
catastrophe	mishap
crash	paroxysm
debacle	tragedy
disaster	upheaval

...and objectively analyzing them without wishful thinking.

Sometimes, it's best to set aside dealing with your misfortune immediately and go back to it a week, a few weeks, or a month later, depending on the situation. By then, your original emotions will have settled down, and you can see what happened in a more objective manner. For example, I remember when my first book on options was published in 1975, I proudly brought it to my parents. They were delighted to see the book, especially because it was dedicated to them.

Everything was serene until the end of the weekend when my father found out my book didn't have a bibliography. He immediately began to berate me for that and said no quality book was ever published without a bibliography.

I was crushed. I felt numb. However, a week later, I could finally bring myself to evaluate his reaction without emotion and applied "Get Real."

- My father was a professor, and all the books he read or published were academic treatises, which had to include a bibliography.
  Then came "Think Positive."
- My book on options was a guide for the lay person to teach them how to make money by using options. I realized I was the pioneer in this field; therefore, my book couldn't have a bibliography.
- Those that followed me into the field would probably cite my book as a source in their bibliographies!
- There was every reason to think I had written a worthwhile book.

The book immediately became so successful that it went through countless printings, had four editions, made the New York Times best-seller list in the business category, and was finally translated into Chinese. All without a bibliography! (My wife was even told decades later by a grad of Harvard Business School that my book was required reading in the finance class.) After this first book, I decided to write two more books on options in 1981 and 1983. This is how I became the go-to guru on options trading, regularly appearing on CNN and Bloomberg.

As I think back, perhaps I shouldn't have been so surprised at my father's negativity to my first book since I had heard a "funny" story about the early days of my parents' marriage. It seems something that my mother cooked was not up to my father's expectations, and he promptly let her know about it, whereupon she burst into tears. My father then responded, "I don't know why you're crying, Honey. I don't complain about half the things I could complain about."

So, perhaps my father had a bit of a critical disposition to start with.

Chapter 3:
The Three Great Rules

"If the only prayer you ever say in your entire life is thank you, it will be enough."

– Meister Eckhardt (German Catholic theologian, philosopher, and mystic)

(1260 – 1328)

Rules.

To be honest, nobody really likes to listen to them, not to speak of following. And I'm going to talk about three rules. Sounds scary, right?

My rules, however, are concise and effective, and the best part is that they'll help you be happy within.

So, the greatest rules for happiness I have ever come across are also the shortest. That doesn't make them any less profound or powerful. I first heard them in a sermon at the All Souls Unitarian Church in New York City. Here they're:

Want what you have.
Do what you can.
Be the best you are.

These principles may seem very simple, but each one is very complex, as we shall see in this chapter. What is important to us is that they can lead to tremendous improvements in almost every aspect of your life. Once you start working with them for a while, they can literally change your life from the one you're leading today to a life filled with joy and enthusiasm. And these rules won't only increase your level of happiness, but they will also help you:

- Make more friends.
- Improve your relations with your co-workers.
- Mold you into a more successful human being as you begin to adopt a completely new outlook on your life.

Rule Number One: Want What You Have.

> "I can't change the direction of the wind, but I can adjust my sails to always reach my destination."
>
> *— Jimmy Dean, country music singer (1928 - 2010)*

This first rule is a bit of a surprise because practically all the advice Americans receive on how to be successful and happy is concerned with getting what they want. The unstated assumption, of course, is that "what you want" means only those things you want <u>that you do not already have.</u> Actually, there are a great many things we want that we already have, but if someone were to ask you to list ten things that you want, you wouldn't think of listing those.

The rule "Want what you have" switches that assumption around and tells you to "Want what you already have now," which is the exact opposite of what we've been hearing all our lives. We have particularly been hearing it from advertisers in all the media.

In fact, almost the entire message of the American advertising industry is that if you buy the product or service that they're advertising, you'll attain some goal which you already have, such as to have more fun or to enjoy the lifestyle of the rich and famous. One of the best at this is Ralph Lauren, with his beautiful color photographs of well-dressed, attractive people enjoying a family outing at their horse farm or 15-room mansion on the ocean. People looking at these photos are likely to say to themselves, "This is the way that I would live if

I could afford it, and this is the way that I would want my family to look."

How does one live like that and look like that? The obvious answer is that you and your family can look like these professional models simply by buying the Ralph Lauren Polo clothing, which is being worn in the advertisement. The advertiser knows that long before you saw this advertisement, you were a social climber, perhaps not an overt one, but nonetheless a closet climber who wouldn't mind being at home in a large Bezos-like compound on the Cape with several very attractive members of the opposite sex lounging around. The advertisers then seek to make the connection between this longing that you already have and their products. Instantly without knowing anything about the clothing, you decide that this is what you want.

Actually, buying one of the sports jackets, which you saw in the advertisement, is not going to make you a member of the "old money" set. Rather it'll make you the very same person you already are, but now you'll be wearing an expensive and admittedly rather attractive sports jacket. If you can afford the jacket, there's no harm done. But what if the jacket isn't exactly within your clothing budget? Or what if you're house hunting and saw a similar type of ad in your paper for a large house in an upscale section of town that you couldn't come close to affording?

The result would be to produce a longing for something you can't have. And this, of course, leads to a sense of frustration and antipathy, which creates unhappiness.

If you asked someone who was longing for an elegant sports jacket what would make them happy, they would tell you that if they just earned a certain amount more a year, they could afford to dress exactly the way they wanted to, and then they would be happy. However, this material craving usually doesn't end with just a sports jacket. In fact, it can go on and on.

The person who is buying a "previously owned" Ford or Chevy wishes they could afford a new one. The person buying a new one may be wishing that they could afford a Lincoln or a Cadillac, and so it goes on until you get to a Rolls Royce. Perhaps, you're so wealthy that many of your friends already have a Rolls? If this is the case, then you can have yours gold-plated like the King of Brunei did for each of his numerous wives.

The person buying a Lincoln could be quite unhappy because they can't quite make the payments on the big Mercedes or BMW. The ones who are buying those cars may really like to be seen in a Rolls Royce, Bentley, or whatever. And when they do acquire those cars, they aren't really living in style unless they have their own full-time chauffeur.

It finally reaches the point where some of the super-rich are vying with one another to see who can afford the fastest and most expensive yacht. Right now, it looks as if the winner might be Larry Ellison, founder of the Oracle database company and an America's Cup winner. If he does get some joy out of his ownership, is it really due to the intrinsic joy of owning a boat, or is it from the fact that he can say to himself, "This yacht proves that I really am one of the most successful businessmen in the world?"

By telling us the rule "Want what we have," we can turn these traditional mindsets upside down. Now, you're not looking at the advertisements to tell you what you need and want, rather now you're looking at what you already have and thinking to yourself, "Wow, am I lucky to have so much!" Everyone reading this book has or owns a virtually infinite number of things, particularly intangibles. Intangibles include having relationships with all the people you know. How valuable to you are your friendships?

Think of it this way. If one of your good friends should happen to die, how much would it be worth to you to be able to bring them back to life? Whatever your answer is, that is the value of something you now have for free. How lucky can you be? How important is the love you give and receive from your relatives? What about the fact that you have your health (even if not perfect)? Isn't that what you really want? You also have the ability to read as well as do so many other activities, which bring you pleasure. If you could realize how much you want those things which you already have, you could be much happier than many billionaires who don't "Want what they have" because they're totally focused on wanting what they don't have.

A few years ago, I was visiting Douglas and Patti Pierson and their three children in Burlington, Vermont.

They were a wonderful family, which I had known for years, and I told them about this rule. Then the youngest of the daughters said to me, "You say we should want what we have, but I have so little." I looked at her in the pink of health and the peak of her youth, and all I could think of was that if she knew how many people would give anything they owned to be able to go back in time and be her age again, she would never say how little she has.

She had the complete love of her parents and grandparents, she had the joy of being with her brothers and sisters, she had her perfect health, and she had the promise of a truly wonderful future. If only she could have appreciated all that she had!

We all have so much that it's almost absurd to list it all. You know you're going to have a healthy breakfast tomorrow (and if you don't, it's not because you can't afford one but just that you don't want to take the time for it or swallow the calories), and the same goes for lunch and dinner. You have a roof over your head, a place to sleep, and adequate bathroom facilities.

The point, however, is not that you have more or less than other people because there'll always be some people who have less than you and others who have more than you. The only exception will be if you happen to be the wealthiest person in America. And if you're Elon Musk, who at the time of writing this is said to be the richest person in the U.S., we really wonder if that would make you the happiest person in the world. You might be, but you might not.

The real point is that you have more than enough to be happy about if only you'll look at it in a positive manner. For instance, instead of saying to yourself that you have a crummy job, think of all the things your job does for you. The first thing it does for you is the obvious one of paying you an income. Without that, where would you be? Perhaps, you couldn't even exist very long without the income from that "crummy" job, so why not appreciate what that income means to you.

Second, many jobs provide very meaningful social contacts. Large companies are worlds of their own with every type of person, and many long-lasting friendships are made in them, to say nothing of a growing number of marriages. That's a very important point to be thankful for, and even in a small company, you probably spend more time during each workday talking with the people you work with than with any other group, including perhaps even your own family.

The third benefit is that you may be receiving a large part of your identity from your job. When people ask you what you do, are you proud to say that you work for one of the biggest companies around? Or do you point out with some pride that you're the lead person in your section? Or that your employer is the best in your state?

Fourth is a point which you may not have thought of, but which should be important to you, and that is that no matter what your job is, you're ultimately helping other people. This is obvious for many occupations such as teachers, doctors, or social workers. But all jobs are ultimately serving someone or some people, just not quite as directly. If you weren't helping someone in some way, then no one would be paying you.

Even if you work in the internal accounting department of a large corporation, what you're doing is important for the company. And the company is serving its customers, who are either people or companies that are owned by people. It's also important for your company's shareholders who have invested in the company and whose retirement may be dependent upon the continuing success of the company. So, you too are helping other people in several ways.

I believe that it doesn't do any good to try to change your emotions, such as being happy or being discouraged, because you can't think yourself into having an emotion. But you can direct your thoughts anywhere you want. So, here's a chance to direct your thoughts away from all the things you want to get and think about how lucky you are to have everything that you do have. For a couple of weeks, why not stop wanting what you don't have and "Want What You Have."

Rule Number Two: Do What You Can

This may seem obvious at first, but once you start thinking about it, it's not quite so easy. "Do what you can." may initially just sound like a pop psychology phrase similar to "You can do anything you want to if you just try hard enough." But "Do What You Can." is very different and far more realistic because it forces you to make some serious limitations on what you do. It's definitely not saying that "What a person can conceive, they can achieve." Of course, that phrase is total nonsense. It has become so popular not because it's true but because it's so positive and hopeful that many people want to believe it. However, that still doesn't make it true.

Unfortunately, it isn't long before people find out that it's pure make-believe. You or I could decide that we wanted to be the next President of the United States, but do you think that we could do it no matter how hard we tried? Of course not.

"Do What You Can." is almost the opposite of "You can accomplish anything if you really try hard enough." because it's saying that you should only attempt to do those things that you believe you have a possibility of being able to do. This means that you won't waste your time and energy on things that you know very well you can't do. For example, saying, "I want to be the richest person in America." is out of the question for 99.9% of the readers of this book, and for the other 0.01%, it's no more likely than winning the $100,000,000 lottery jackpot. Anyone attempting this foolish goal is doomed to disappointment and heartbreak.

It could be that by trying to become the richest person in America, you would work very ably at your own occupation and become very successful even if you didn't achieve your stated goal of becoming the richest person in the country. This could be a wonderful achievement for you, but it wouldn't be because you tried to become the richest person in the country, but rather because you set out to excel at your job. In other words, your stated goal of becoming the richest person in the world contained a lesser goal of succeeding in your job, and that lesser goal is what made you a success.

"Do What You Can." is a realistic motto, which requires you to ask yourself a very important question before you do anything. That question is just "what can you do?" In this book, we describe many things you can do to make your life, and that of the people around you, a better life. Things like calling someone you haven't talked to in weeks or months. Or joining an organization devoted to people who have interests like yours, such as skiing, gardening, helping the disadvantaged, or practicing and developing your spirituality. Joining these organizations are just some of the projects that "You can do."

If you love to ski and you can find a skier club in your area, they'll probably welcome you with open arms, and you could have many wonderful times and make a great many good friends through that club. If, on the other hand, your consuming goal is to become an Olympic downhill skiing champion, then you better think carefully before you give up your daytime job. At the least, it'd help if you were the number one skier in your high school, college, or country. Remember, "Do What You Can." is not the same as "do what you wish you could do."

These are extreme examples, but in real life, this phrase will give rise to some serious soul searching. Let's say you want to purchase a larger home. You decide that you could afford to make the purchase, but the question you have is whether you'll be able to afford the ongoing expenses after you buy it, such as the continuing costs of the mortgage payments, electricity, real estate taxes, oil, or gas heat, insurance, maintenance, and miscellaneous.

This problem may be challenging, but it can be resolved by good budgeting. So, figuring out whether you can afford this home is a problem you can resolve. You make up a budget for your future expenses and compare that number to your anticipated income. Some decisions are more difficult because they involve intangibles such as relationships.

Let's say you're a member of a two-career household with one spouse earning more than the other, but both are contributing in a meaningful way to supporting the household. One of the spouses receives an offer from an employer in another town about 200 miles away at a significantly higher salary. Do you accept the offer? If you do, then living together during the week is out of the question. Even to get together every weekend would either be expensive or require a long drive through stretches of heavy traffic.

"Do What You Can." may seem to be telling you that, of course, you can do it. So, you'll be separated for most of each week, but, hey, life isn't without its inconveniences, and the money would really come in handy. So, you can do it, but this rule doesn't mean that you should do everything which is physically possible for you to do. What it implies is that you should do everything you can, which will have an overall positive impact on your life.

A somewhat similar example would be if you're working at a full-time job and you find out about a part-time job that would require working four hours in the evening, four days a week. Should you take it? You're strong and physically fit, and you could do the job and still get enough sleep. So, a literal reading of this rule would seem to indicate a positive response. But just because you could actually do it and survive doesn't mean that you should do it.

The real question is whether you can do the extra job and still have the time to do so many other things that add to your overall well-being. If taking on the extra job means that you'll have no time to relax or enjoy yourself, then the fact that you physically could do the job isn't as important as what it'll do to your total life experience. If, on the other hand, you have a specific financial goal, such as earning enough money so that you can attempt to climb Mt. Kilimanjaro, and you could take on this job for three months which would earn enough to pay for the trip, then that's a different story.

We said that you can't order your brain to become happy because we can't create emotional states on command. However, there's a great number of specific commands that we can tell our brain to do. If I said to you, "I want you to think of President George Washington," you would immediately think of a man with a white wig, perhaps crossing the Delaware River in a small boat with a band of soldiers and a large American flag. Thus, we learn that it's very easy to direct our brain to do certain things, such as recalling images, which are stored there. However, we can't command our brains to create emotions, such as happiness, love, or anger. Directing our brain to take the kind of orders it can carry out is another method of taking action just as surely as telephoning someone is, and it can have just as significant consequences.

"Do what you can." requires you to make a realistic assessment of what the likely or possible outcomes will be of the action you're contemplating. You don't have to decline a certain course of action just because you can't be sure of the outcome. After all, nothing is certain in this world. It's enough that you believe you have a reasonable chance of having a positive outcome. If everyone had to be absolutely certain of everything they did, there would be no weather forecasts. The entire occupation of stockbrokers would disappear overnight because they persuade people to buy a stock they believe will go up, but they don't actually **know** if it will go up or down.

Let's say your spouse has been doing something that is really annoying you, and you want to talk with him/her about it. Now, consider the following possibilities:

- What are the chances that you'll succeed in getting the change you want?
- What are the chances that they'll say they won't change?
- What are the chances that not only will they say that they won't change but that because you were so insensitive as to ask them to change something that they really want to continue doing, they're going to do it even more just to show you that you're not their boss?

It may be impossible for you to answer this question with any degree of accuracy because predicting another person's reactions is always fraught with danger. Nevertheless, this is the kind of intellectual exercise that you should go through before you set off on any major activity. Many times, by just thinking about the possible outcomes, you'll have an idea of how you can improve the outcome by changing your action. In this case, instead of saying, "You know dear, it really annoys me when you __________, and I wish you would stop," you could ask a question first such as, "Do you realize that you often ____________, and I was wondering if you knew you were doing it so often?"

But of course, the main theme of this rule is not to spend an inordinate amount of time wondering if you can do it, but rather to get going and do it. "Do what you can." is a positive rule because there are literally thousands of things you can do to make yourself happier by improving your relations with other people, by giving yourself more structured recreation time, by getting more sleep, having more time to relax, pursuing your hobbies, etc. It's basically an exhortation to get out of your armchair in front of the TV or the internet and start doing things you can be proud of. There's an almost infinite number of pleasurable things you can do, and this rule is telling you to start doing them, now!

Rule Number Three: "Be the Best You Are."

Like the other two rules, this one seems very easy at first. Of course, we're going to be who we're, and in fact, no matter what we do, it's an expression of who we're. As Polonius told us in Shakespeare's Hamlet, "This above all, to thine own self be true."

Whether we go out and get drunk or write an award-winning poem, we can find something in our past that we can link to our activities and conclude that what we did was expressing a part of our own selves. But to get any benefit from this rule, we must focus on a certain part of who we're, and that part is the part that is most likely to lead to our goal of happiness.

It's true that almost no matter what we do, it's an expression of who we are. But if we're telling ourselves to be who we are, what are we trying to accomplish? It seems clear that we're trying to be the best of who we are because that is the way we're going to find happiness. One could argue that because we like to take vacations, that if we were to quit our job and devote ourselves to constant traveling around the world, we would be acting out who we are. But is that really what we want to do? There're so many facets to our lives that we could do almost anything and find that we're "being who we are."

The best interpretation of this phrase is that we want to carry out the best aspect of who we are. We have all done things that we're proud of and regrettably done some things we're ashamed of. They're all a part of who we are. But if we're to adopt a rule that is to be helpful to us in guiding our lives, then it must be a rule that will enable us to improve our lives. Therefore, the real meaning of this rule is "Be the best of who you already are." A similar common phrase is, "Be the best you possibly can."

However, this is too open-ended because no one knows what the best they possibly can be is. Our rule is easier to follow because it's only asking you to do things that are already a part of your core. If you're always honest, then when you answer a question truthfully, you're "to thine own self being true," and if you lie, you're not being "true to thine own self" and you won't be happy about it.

It may seem like a cliché, but it's far from that. What it means is that we must still concentrate on looking into ourselves and decide what we're all about. And then, when we have discovered that, we must bring our attention to the best parts of ourselves and encourage those traits in the future. Let's say that one part of your life is that you have a lot of friends and feel very good about that part of your life. As we note elsewhere in this book, friends are of the utmost importance, and spending time with them is one of the best things that we can do with our lives. But what if you're spending too much time partying? That's possible too.

The rule "Be the Best You are." can remind you of all that you are. You may also be a parent and perhaps the financial provider for your family. Are you spending so much time going to club functions, hanging out at the local sports bar, playing golf, or taking vacations that you're neglecting some of these other aspects of who you really are?

Even your friendships could perhaps benefit from some reflections on who you really are. Some of your friendships are more meaningful to you than others simply because you feel more comfortable talking about significant topics with that person. Do your conversations with this person provide a fairly accurate description of who you really are? Are you a person who enjoys a serious discussion about a meaningful topic?

Not everyone does. I know people who never discuss politics, economics, or religion because it's just too stressful and arouses too many emotions. If that is who you really are, then you know that you want to continue to cultivate people who have a lot of "fun" and don't want to "waste" their time, for example, worrying about the impact on the next generation of long-term global warming.

But if you're concerned about topics such as the mounting Federal budget deficit and what its effect will be on our economy in the coming decades, then you owe it to yourself to spend time with people who also are concerned about this looming problem. This is just another example of, "To thine own self be true."

In the real world, decisions are often not that easy, especially if there's a conflict between different "good" sides of who you're. Suppose you take pride in being a good father, and this Thursday evening, your daughter has an important game, which can decide who goes to the state tournament. Of course, you want to be there. On the other hand, your club is having its once-a-year fundraiser that same night, and you have always shown your loyalty to the club by attending the event, as do almost all members.

Unfortunately, there's no happy solution to this dilemma. You must decide which of these parts of you is more important to you on this evening. Is it being the caring parent, or is it being the reliable club supporter? The question to ask yourself is, "Which part of you is the real you and represents the best part of you?" If someone were to ask you what your real core "you" would be, would your answer be that it's being a loyal club member who is known for always supporting the club, or would it be that you're proud to be a great father for your wonderful daughter? Is it more important for you to support the club or your daughter? Only you can decide, but at least you can decide based upon some solid reasoning rather than just guessing whom you'll disappoint the least.

Each one of us has been on this earth for a good amount of time, and during that period, we have gotten to know ourselves pretty well. We have a good idea of who we really are. We know:

- What turns us on.
- What aggravates us.
- What bores us.
- What makes us feel good or bad.
- What kind of people we like and what kind we don't.
- What we like to do.
- What we wouldn't be caught dead doing.

So, when you come to a fork in the road, just reach into yourself and pick the one which best expresses your core values.

We can all remember things we have done that represent the best part of ourselves. Good deeds we have performed such as aiding a friend in need, visiting an ailing relative, being a companion to someone who was lonely, contributing to a charity, working extra hard to help our boss, or skimping on our standard of living so that our children could go to college.

In my own case, one of my actions, which has brought me the most satisfaction, is when I found out that a newly widowed relative had been denied social security by the government, which she had been counting on. At the time, I was a tax lawyer, and I came up with a plan for her to pay a relatively small amount of additional money to the IRS, which legitimately allowed her to receive social security benefits for the rest of her life.

With all your history, you'll eventually come up with an answer of what you should do to truly "Be who you are," with an emphasis on the best part of who you're.

The result will be very satisfactory. As Ayn Rand noted, "Happiness is that state of mind which occurs not so much when you think of your possessions, and not even from your accomplishments, but from the achievement of your own values." Only you know what they are and perhaps you should think about them to learn more clearly exactly what they are. You can always gain happiness by living according to your own best values, which is another way of saying, "Be the best of who you're."

In the next chapters, we'll explore how to apply these rules to many of the specific situations you may encounter in your everyday life. We'll start with a chapter explaining what happiness is so that you'll know what your goal should be from reading this book.

Chapter 4:
What Is Happiness?

Remember that happiness is a way of travel – not a destination.

– Roy M Goodman, New York State Senator, 1930-2014

We need to know what happiness is if we're going to learn how to attain it, and just as importantly, to know when we have attained it. In our journey to happiness, just like any other journey, we must know what our destination is if we expect to have any hope of finding it.

Happiness is enjoying life to the fullest.

It means truly believing that you're a very lucky person to be born who you are.

It means appreciating the many aspects of your life, which you love.

Happy people are happy with their spouses or significant others, with their parents, and with their children. They actually enjoy their work or at least accept it as a great way to provide for their material needs. They have interests outside themselves, which they enjoy doing for relaxation or recreation, and which fill them with enthusiasm and joy. Happy people also appreciate that they have wonderful friends and that they're extremely lucky to have them.

Happy people aren't overly concerned about what others think about them; they're more concerned about what they think about themselves, and they're determined to do everything in their power to live up to their highest expectations of themselves. They enjoy material possessions but don't judge their worth as human beings by what they own, but rather by how successful they're in accomplishing their goals. Often, their goals involve activities that end up helping other people.

They're concerned about the welfare of other people and spend a significant part of their lives doing things that help others. Happy people are content with themselves and accept responsibility for their lives. Their happiness is independent of whether they're having a good day, whether they can earn over $250,000 this year, whether their children will be in the top 10% of their class, whether they'll marry someone whom all their friends will admire, and whether everyone is always going to like them.

I'm very lucky because I had an excellent example of a very happy person right in my family. A few years ago, when my father was 95 years old, I talked with him about happiness. He was a great man; he was outstanding in his field of Adlerian psychology, but by age 95, the very close friends he grew up with and continued seeing throughout his life had passed on. His four sons visited him regularly, but the closest one lived 200 miles away, and there were weeks between visits when he was basically alone with a caretaker. My mother, who had been his adoring wife and companion for 65 years, had recently died. He was very hard of hearing, and his reluctance to wear a hearing aid meant that it could be difficult to have a conversation with him. This also contributed to his being alone much of the time. His memory was failing, he was walking more slowly, and because of his poor hearing and eyesight, the State Motor Vehicle Department had just revoked his driver's license.

He had dozens of other smaller problems, which he could have seized upon as reasons to be unhappy.

And there are many elderly people in this country who do exactly that—spending a great deal of their time complaining. They feel fully justified in complaining about the lack of attention they get from their children, about their health problems, their inability to do what they used to, about the constantly rising prices, or what a dismal life they're leading.

Yet when I asked my father if he was happy, he didn't utter a single complaint but said, "Yes, of course, I am." And then, looking directly at me and beaming a big smile, he said, "But that's because I have so much to be happy about."

He was happy about his four sons, all of whom had turned out well. He was proud of what he had done with his life, which included having edited, with my mother, what is still the standard book presenting the work of the seminal early psychologist Alfred Adler. Perhaps even more importantly, he dearly loved the present.

He got a deep enjoyment out of watching the traffic go by on the busy street in the front of our house and watching the neighbors walking or driving up our little Bilodeau Court by the side of the house. In the summer, he could sit out on the porch and observe both views, and in the winter, he could see almost as well through the picture windows of the living room. He was content and relaxed after a long and hard-working life.

How can we reach the same state that my father was in then? Unfortunately, you can't go directly to happiness. It's like trying to fall in love or trying to fall out of love, but you can do things that will promote happiness. No book by itself can bring you happiness, but it can lead you onto a path so that you can bring happiness to yourself. In this book, I'll explain what true happiness is and contrast it with pleasure.

I'll show you how you can use pleasure to lead yourself to happiness. I'll share with you exercises of various activities, which can lead you directly to the door of happiness. These include exercises such as how to get out of a blue mood with a very detailed step-by-step progression, starting with something as simple as just breathing and eventually leading to major contributions you can make to your happiness as well as the happiness of others. These steps don't require any superhuman willpower or exertions.

They're designed to accomplish three goals at the same time.

The first is to give you something positive to do. In other words, the very fact that you're doing something constructive, which is aimed at helping yourself, is going to make you feel better if for no other reason than that it takes your mind off what has been making you unhappy.

The second goal they're designed to accomplish is something that is worthwhile for its own sake. For example, studies of people who're happy have shown that one of the basic characteristics most of them have is that they have interactions with many people. So, a principal purpose of many of the exercises in this book is to involve you with other people, which in itself can create more happiness in your life.

The third goal is that these exercises will contribute to the most difficult aspect of happiness of all. That is to change your mind from thinking that the most important thing in the world is what has been happening to you. What has been happening to you is almost by definition totally passive on your part, meaning that you may have little control over it. Often, these external events are perceived as being negative. Examples are; my professor gave me a low mark on the first exam, my girlfriend/ boyfriend doesn't seem to be paying as much attention to me as he/she used to, my boss didn't give me as big a raise as I expected, this damn arthritis is getting worse every year, etc.

If anyone were to concentrate on the negative things that are happening in their lives, it would naturally make them unhappy. What needs to happen is to shift your focus to believe that the most important thing in the world is the great amount of happiness you can receive from doing things for and with other people. This doesn't mean just charity; it also means how you can make the lives of other people around you better. Just interacting more with them on a social level is all that is often required to both make others happier and to get you out of thinking so much about yourself.

Look around you at anyone you consider happy, and you'll find that they have strong interests outside themselves that they consider far more important than the problems which they themselves have. So, the third benefit of these exercises is that they will change the focus of your life from inward, which can mean focusing on your negative thoughts, to outward, where you're becoming an active participant in worthy pursuits.

One example of these exercises is the simple technique of asking yourself the right questions. The reason this is important is that our brains are like computers; if you want information from a computer, you have to ask it a question or make a request for exactly what you want. The computer will then give you the information you have requested; if you ask the wrong question, you won't get the information you wanted. If you want information from your brain, you ask it a question, and the answer you get will depend upon the question you ask.

Let's say that something has just gone wrong. Naturally, you'll feel upset, and perhaps you're also feeling that you've failed and that nothing is going right today. If you ask yourself a question that will lead to a negative answer, you can expect to have your negative thoughts reinforced. For example, if you ask, "How come I fail at almost everything I do?" your brain will come up with an answer to that question.

Since we just asked our brain why something negative has happened, it will have to give us an answer that is negative. Our brain may answer by telling us that we're often a failure because we're really not very smart, and/or we're afraid to push our point of view with others, or we can't think quick enough, or we're too lazy, or we don't come from the right background, or we've just been unlucky since the day we were born, etc.

Obviously, the effect of these answers is only to reinforce a belief that you're indeed a failing person whom the world is consistently attacking for good reasons. With thoughts like these rushing through your head, is it any wonder that you could feel doomed to failure before you even begin to do anything? And, of course, this sense of failure may also include a conclusion that the world is really against you. Such feedback is virtually guaranteed to make your life even more unproductive and unhappy.

If, on the other hand, you ask yourself questions that seek positive information, the effect can be tremendously uplifting. For instance, the next time you have a disappointment, you could ask yourself, "What can I learn from this experience which will enable me to do better the next time this happens?" Your brain will answer this question with some insights that may surprise you. You'll be proud of the ideas that can come out of your own brain. By the way, you don't necessarily have to settle for the first answer.

Ask your brain, "And what else can I do?" or "What can I do to be even more successful?" Each time you ask another question, your brain will strive to come up with another answer. These answers will give you important guidance that you can use to improve your life and bring you that much closer to happiness. This exercise is just one example of the many you'll find in this book.

I've made an effective combination of practical exercises that will begin working immediately when you perform them to make you a happier person. Also, I have included descriptions of some of the attitudes happy people have, which you can use to convert your attitudes from those which unhappy people have toward those outlooks found in happy people.

If you lead the same kind of life that happy people lead, you too will become happy. After all, if it looks like a duck, acts like a duck, and quacks like a duck, we conclude that it's a duck. If you act like happy people do, think like happy people do, and do it consistently, you too will become a happy person.

In the next chapter, I'll introduce you to pleasure, which is the sister of happiness and shares many of her characteristics, although she's quite different. We'll explore these differences and let you decide which one you would like to marry.

Chapter 5: The Difference Between Pleasure and True Happiness

"Pleasure is always derived from something outside you, whereas joy arises from within."

– Eckhart Tolle, author, "The Power of Now" German teacher, (1948 – Present)

Have you ever come home from a wonderful vacation where you spent a full two weeks just having a truly great time? You traveled to a country where you were able to really relax, enjoy the fascinating people, the scenery, the world-famous food, and all in an atmosphere of fun, relaxation, and enjoyment.

Maybe the trip was a luxurious cruise with all the comforts that one can imagine.

Maybe it was a trip to France with at least two meals a day that was just out of this world.

Maybe it was a camping trip to a National Park with breathtaking scenery.

Maybe your vacation was in the middle of the winter, and you happily left the gray skies and snow of your home for the bright, hot sun and sandy beaches of Florida or the Caribbean.

Whatever the case, you're returning, sun-tanned, well-fed, fully relaxed, and with fond thoughts of a memorable two weeks and hundreds of photos to prove it. It was all just like a scene from Travel and Leisure Magazine.

And then something totally surprising happens. There's a minor hitch in getting out of the airport, or one of the kids has a complaint, or something is out of place when you get home, and suddenly you're yelling at your spouse in a tone of voice that you usually reserve for a serious problem. Your spouse shouts back at you with the same amount of anger in their voice. You're stunned by the vehemence and anger in your own voice, and the amount of anger that you feel inside of yourself over what you recognize is a minor annoyance. How could this happen? Here you are, sun-tanned, happy, relaxed, and feeling in a great mood. Suddenly, your entire mood changes from one of being super relaxed to one of anger and even outrage at what's happening.

The answer to this question is that you've had two weeks of extreme pleasure, but you weren't necessarily having two weeks of extreme happiness.

If you could be standing on the deck of your cruise ship, watching the sunset in a melody of colors, with a delightful Mimosa in your hand, as the ship pulled slowly out of port onto the tropical blue sea, you were experiencing pleasure. And you translated this in your mind into perfect happiness. When you got home and exploded at the first minor setback that occurred, you were astounded that all the good feelings, which you had been collecting for the past two weeks, didn't come through and solve this tiny inconvenience. And that's one difference between pleasure and happiness.

Pleasure is frequently associated with our senses. You see a beautiful sight. You smell a sweet flower or perhaps a pungent roast cooking in your oven. You feel the physical closeness of a loved one. You taste a rare 2000 vintage Bordeaux wine. In all these cases, your senses are sending your brain messages that are designed to make you feel good.

Your senses are telling you in the strongest language they have that whatever you're doing is OK and that you should continue doing whatever you're doing. When you've just finished dining on an excellent dinner, you feel satisfied, full, and comfortable. Your body is telling you that it's good to eat, and your senses are encouraging you to eat again so that you won't starve to death.

However, your enjoyment of all these senses can give you a temporary feeling of well-being without making you truly happy. The reason is that our physical senses aren't what determine whether we humans are happy. A well-known example is that two lovers can be very happy just being with each other even if they're shivering in the rain, freezing at a ski resort, or starving at midnight because they didn't have time to grab dinner.

One clue to this distinction is that senses are not even an exclusively human feature. Think of the moods that cats have. They have plenty of senses too. Your cat is very contented after it has had its dinner and very pleased to find the warmest part of your house in the winter and sit right on it. Can we say that cats are really happy? We may believe that they are because we tend to humanize them, but there's little evidence that they're happy, only that they're now enjoying sensations that are comfortable for them.

If we look at the opposite of pleasurable sensations, we can learn a bit more about these pleasures. The opposite of sensory pleasure is pain or discomfort. For instance, if you eat some bad food, you might develop a very unpleasant stomach ache, and this could easily make you unhappy.

On the other hand, it might not make you unhappy at all. You might be very happy because this is the day you're getting married, about to start a new job, or go on a vacation, which you have been looking forward to for weeks.

In these cases, you might say that you're unhappy. You would probably simply say that your stomach hurts and that you want to take some antacid pills right away, but it wouldn't really make you unhappy because your state of happiness is built upon something which is truly important to you, and that genuine human feeling can often overcome the negative impact of an upset stomach.

When we experience only sensory messages, it's just the opposite, in that they can be easily trumped by our sense of happiness or unhappiness. If you just had a loved one who died, you might not even be interested in having a wonderful dinner. No matter what delightful sensations you experienced, they wouldn't be able to change your feeling of intense sadness.

Pleasure comes from sensual and other enjoyments, such as a good dinner, an intense movie, or a truly relaxing massage. These give us lovely sensations, but they're only temporary in nature. This is what most advertisements are selling, and it's relatively easy to attain. Is your life too dull? Then buy a fast new car. Bored with eating? Try a new recipe, etc. Want someone to love you? Get the sophisticated new perfume just being introduced at a very high price. These material improvements in your life are unlikely to lead to lasting happiness.

Just think of the former ruler of Egypt, King Farouk, who devoted his later years to a life of debauchery. He had a tremendous amount of money, not much to do with his time, and a distinct liking for women, good food, and good liquor, not necessarily in that order. According to a biography of him, although from an early age he had thousands of acres of land, dozens of palaces, and hundreds of cars, he was never satisfied with his wealth, and in fact, took to stealing items from his subjects and even from heads of state whom he visited. He ate so much that when he died, he weighed almost 300 pounds. Does this sound like a happy person?

He certainly didn't look that way. He became even fatter as the years passed on and even less interested in most of the things that had formerly given him pleasure. In fact, you don't have to leave the United States to find examples of people who may seem to have everything that can make them happy, but somehow, they don't really seem to be happy.

One good domestic example is the late Hugh Heffner of Playboy Magazine fame. If you have read Playboy or just skimmed through it at your barbershop, you always saw Hugh surrounded by beautiful, tall, buxom blondes with lovely smiles. Do you think that after all these years of posing with his Playmates, he was really going to be made happy by having a photoshoot with another one?

Not unless he had failed to let his human maturation continue beyond the age of 19. What satisfaction could he have gotten from posing with these women when he knew full well that the only reason the women were doing it was that they were trying to get some free publicity so they could enhance their careers in modeling or acting. Could it possibly have boosted his ego to be used by these women? Did he realize that if he weren't Hugh Heffner but just someone with another name who acted, sounded, and looked exactly like Hugh Heffner, there probably wouldn't have been a single playmate who would even have given him a second look? You can bet that Hugh knew it too.

The distinction between happiness and pleasure is that pleasure often comes from the outside. Think of travel, movies, a great concert, or enjoying some wonderful chocolates. Happiness comes from the inside and reflects contentment and inner serenity, which makes it possible to enjoy just being alive and to enjoy almost anything external.

True happiness can, therefore, be an intellectual state of mind, and the more one thinks about it, the happier one can become. You're happy because of who you are, what you've done, who your friends are, your relationships with your relatives, and in many cases, what you're doing or have done in your career and the wonderful people whom you have met throughout your life.

Pleasure is, of course, something which we can look forward to, and it's an essential part of life. The amount of money that's spent today in the United States on entertainment and media is absolutely staggering—$203 billion a year. Incidentally, that's almost three times what's spent on education. People crave entertainment and are willing to spend huge amounts, as in the case of concerts by top rock bands, which can have tickets up to as much as $20,000. The restaurants in large cities that have the highest prices often have the most customers.

And yet, no matter how wonderful the food in a restaurant is, once the meal is over, there's nothing, except perhaps a memory and a charge on the next credit card bill. A rough analogy of the differences between pleasure and happiness exists in jewelry as the difference between costume jewelry and the authentic article.

If all you want is to impress other people and to have bragging rights because you're wearing something on your finger that looks very expensive, then costume jewelry may do the job. Of course, you know that it's a fake, and every time you look at it, you'll be reminded that you're trying to fool other people into thinking that you're more affluent than you really are.

Can this be a source of true happiness for you? I would suggest that it wouldn't. Also, there's nothing there of lasting value. If you ever wish to sell it or leave it to your heirs, they'll quickly discover that it's a fake and that you've been living your life with this little white lie. Not a happy thought. A piece of real jewelry, no matter how small, can give you lasting enjoyment as you contemplate that it's a piece of nature that has been in existence for millions of years, that it could increase in value as time goes on, and that it represents something in you which is true and honest.

This is like the difference between pleasure and happiness. For a brief while, pleasure can make you feel good, but because it's externally caused, it may soon disappear and need repeating if it is going to sustain you. Real happiness is internal and comes from a feeling inside that you're leading a worthy life in which your goals aren't only making you happy but can be helping to make many other people happy too. This is the kind of joy that can last a lifetime. That's what true happiness is.

As you go about your life, enjoy the pleasures that life can offer. Who doesn't love chocolate or ice cream? However, remember that they can never replace true happiness, which is locked into your view of the world and of yourself. As long as you have that, you will always have true happiness.

Chapter 6
Thirteen Ways to Lift Your Spirits

"Even if we can't be happy, we must always be cheerful."

– Irving Kristol, American Journalist. (1920-2009)

Whether you are feeling a little blue, terribly sad, or very depressed, what follows in this chapter will show you effective ways to lift your spirits using a mental approach, whereby you contemplate simple pleasures when you're alone and relaxed. In this chapter, I'll focus on mental exercises that you can do by yourself when you're comfortable, relaxed, and can contemplate. As you progress from step to step, your mood will begin to lift, and you'll be ready to take on the action-oriented activities I recommend in Chapters 7 and 8, which in turn will lift your spirits even more.

Let's get started.

Step 1. Remember, all bad moods come to an end.

This first step is vital. Bad moods do come to an end. You know this because your gloominess hasn't been a life-long condition. By just doing a mental review, you should admit to yourself that in the past, when you felt down-in-the-dumps… somehow… sometime… you came out the other end of that long, dark tunnel. Embrace this truth which underscores the fact that humans can endure almost anything if they know it's only temporary.

Research also suggests that many bad moods come to an end quickly and dramatically. You don't lose the feeling of gloominess gradually, but rather you suddenly experience a strong mood change bringing you from feeling blue to a mild burst of more normal happiness. Many have described this feeling "as a dark cloud lifting overhead." Even when you're depressed over a long period of time, you need to remind yourself that the feeling of helplessness and/or hopelessness you may feel now hasn't plagued you every single day of your life 24/7. Keeping this fact in mind can certainly reassure you that the funk you're in now will definitely also come to a happy ending.

Step 2. Take six deep breaths.

When you're feeling very blue, you aren't yourself, and you may be functioning at about 20% of your normal capacity. You need something easy to do since 80% of your resources are out of commission. And that's exactly how easy it is to do this next mental exercise. Remember, the longest journey begins with a single step, and we will make that first step very easy. It starts with the simplest activity of all. Breathing!

Get comfortable in a quiet space. Sit up straight or lie down, whichever is more relaxing for you. Try to find a private, quiet space with no outside stimuli like TV or radio. You're going to clear your mind of other thoughts and feelings and apply a laser-like focus on just your breathing. Inhale through your nose deeply and slowwww-ly. Then exhale through your mouth and push the air out with a big Whoosh. It's important to create a steady rhythm and duplicate it with each subsequent inhale and exhale. Some people say to themselves, "Inhale slowly. Exhale forcefully." Others breathe while simply counting slowly. Breathing in this slow, steady manner helps to reduce the stress and anxiety you have been feeling. Whether you take six breaths to unwind or need 15 minutes is up to you, but you know the dividends it'll yield.

If you want to improve your deep breathing technique, try this out. Breathe normally and put one hand on your chest and the other on your stomach. Think about the hand on your chest. Is it moving in and out? Sure, it is. How about the hand on your stomach? Is it moving? No, but it should be. Natural breathing should involve your diaphragm, which is the large muscle in your abdomen below your belly button.

When you breathe in deeply, you should feel the hand on your belly expand outward. When you expel your breath fully, the hand on your belly should fall inward toward the back of your stomach. Breathe again, so this time you feel the hand on your stomach moving and at the same time notice that the hand on your chest isn't moving like it did in the beginning when you were breathing with shallow breaths. This new kind of breathing is called "belly" breathing and brings in the most oxygen to the body.

Over time, people don't pay attention and forget how to breathe this way and use just their chest and shoulders. This results in short, shallow breaths, which can increase their stress and anxiety. However, singers must learn belly breathing. So do musicians who play wind instruments. And so do regular people who take yoga and Pilates classes. People from all different walks of life can learn this technique; you too can practice and adopt this method of breathing. Why would you bother to relearn how to breathe?

- You learn to relax more fully.
- You de-stress and can reduce your anxiety.

- You live with more joy and less worry.

Deep, slow breathing makes you feel better because more oxygen is going into your brain and enabling it and the rest of your body to work better. By the way, you probably know, one of the main reasons so many people around the world are tobacco smokers is that they get a boost from the nicotine in it.

What you may not know is that a large part of the enjoyment people get from smoking is also because when they smoke, they're automatically inhaling fully to suck in the smoke and then exhaling slowly - and it's this deep breathing that gives smokers a large part of their pleasure! So, when you do the deep breathing exercises, you can understand why smokers consider smoking a satisfying pleasure.

You can achieve that same enjoyment without having to worry about getting lung cancer simply by clearing your mind and taking deep, slow rhythmic breaths. When you breathe in this manner, there's a cascade of benefits for your mind and body:

- Your breathing slows down.
- Then your heart beats more slowly.
- Then your blood pressure decreases.

This exercise is also healthy because oxygen is essential to the sound operation of your body, including your brain. When you're in a depressed mood, even your breathing declines; therefore, you may have been depriving your brain of the oxygen which it needs to function at its peak level.

The bottom line is that "just" breathing slowly and deeply six times can make a world of difference in how you feel. It's also a great initial step to get back to your normal self. While you're doing this exercise, you'll already be accomplishing three things:

- You're doing something positive, and you're exercising your own free will to do it. This is a big victory because it means that the positive, upbeat part of you is fighting back against the depression which has been robbing you of the ability to take control of your actions.
- As you take those six big breaths, you can enjoy the sensation of the air going into your lungs and cleaning out the stale old air which has been bottled up there. Think about the extra oxygen which will soon be flowing into your brain. This could be your first pleasurable thought in a long while.
- When you're finished, you can start to think about which of the many steps outlined below you would like to take to continue on the path to becoming the happy person you expect to become.

When you have finished this exercise, you should congratulate yourself. True, this was a simple exercise, but it was a big first step, and remember that the longest journey starts with but a single step. You have just made that first step. It was an important first which you have successfully accomplished, and it can lead you on your journey back to happiness.

Step 3. Appreciate something small.

One of the common characteristics of being very blue is the urge to retreat from the world. If you're depressed, you might go even further and sleep 10-12 hours a day or just lie in bed most of the day in the fetal position while you doze in and out of unawareness. In short, you're too sad to bear the world. Of course, it's not the world, which is too sad; it's your interpretation of the information you receive that makes you so sad.

That's why so many of our exercises are designed to get you to focus on the wonderful world around you. You may feel sad because you think that your world is an awful place, but compared to other people's lives, it's probably a wonderful life. After all, you aren't enduring the agony of your home burning down and losing all your possessions, living in a Somali refugee camp, or starving in Darfur. Count your blessings!

There are millions of people living in this very same world who are filled with happiness, and you could be one of them too. If only you had a different outlook and different objectives, and that's what this book is about.

Just as depressed people try to block out the world, happier people want to learn and experience as much about it as they can. They're aware of what's happening around them, so they adapt to change and rise to challenges. What we're going to do is to make you also more aware of your world so that you'll feel attached to it, to its energy, to its beauty, and finally to its love. Here's how we get started.

To become aware of the world, we need to forget the concerns we have now—concerns that have made us unhappy, that have disappointed us, that have made us wonder whether our friends are really our friends. We worry that we may not have enough money to last for the rest of our life, whether our health is likely to get worse, and on and on. And so, we're going to start small.

I want you to focus on appreciating small pleasures which can make you feel better. Here are some examples.

- Go into the freezer and scoop out a small portion of ice cream. Take one small spoonful and savor it in your mouth. Hmmm, it gives you immediate pleasure. You taste that wonderful vanilla bean. You can feel the coolness go down your throat. As you appreciate the sensation of eating this wonderful ice cream, tell yourself that you can enjoy ice cream for the rest of your life and that there are many other pleasures ahead for you that are much greater than a few spoonfuls of ice cream. (If you're a compulsive eater, on the other hand, skip this exercise.)
- Look out the window. Focus on something you haven't noticed before. Is there a tree you can see? If so, is it young or old? What species of tree is it? How does it get nourishment into the top leaves? There're a lot of things to appreciate about a tree, i.e., the shade it provides, how it adds to the total appearance of your home, the home it provides for birds and squirrels, and finally, the wood it provides us to build homes, furniture, and stay warm.

- Is there a flower nearby? Go over and look at it for an entire minute. Does it have a fragrance? Appreciate it. Appreciate the delicacy of the petals and the colors. Think of how many colors there're in this flower. What are the names of the colors?

Your first reaction might be, "What good does it do me to see a flower? I'm angry because I just got screwed by my boss, and this stupid flower isn't going to help me one bit." Well, it can do you a lot of good because while you are appreciating the flower (or a tree or ice cream), you won't be seething about your boss. After you've thought about the flower, your thoughts might go back to your boss, but they'll have lost some of their venom. And that has a lot of benefit for you. Remember that by living in the present, you'll automatically push unhappiness out of your mind, unless at that moment you're freezing cold, unbearably hot, starving for something to eat, or in physical pain.

Well, none of those conditions apply to you now, do they? No, they don't because you're very likely to be well-fed and not in physical pain. In fact, you're comfortably seated and relaxed while you're reading this book. So, the point to recognize is that when you're really living in the present, focusing on pleasant thoughts, there's nothing to be unhappy about.

Step 4. Listen to some of your favorite music but not as background music.

This is an easy and fun step. Instead of listening to music while you're multitasking as you usually do, give yourself permission to listen as a solo activity concentrating on the beautiful music just as you would if you were attending a live concert. So, select one of the pieces you like the most in your favorite music app, or tune into your favorite radio station, and then sit down and do nothing except listening! Down with multitasking! Music as therapy is a proven way to de-stress and reduce anxiety. You may not have done it in a while, but you'll see how good it feels.

As part of this exercise, you might be inspired to add to your collection of music, which is a great activity because it's not only fun to think of what you want to get, but you can also enjoy the thought of listening to it in the future.

Step 5. Read a book.

You don't even have to buy one because almost all of us have some wonderful books lying around the house which we really wanted to read when we bought them, but then somehow, we just never had the time to get around to doing so. Go find them now and start one. If you just try, you will find the time.

Step 6. Use the internet to expand your world.

There's so much information available online that you can use to stay informed, shape your opinions and make you a lifelong learner. If you are religious, you can find every denomination represented with programs and sermons that can help you find how to lead a more inspirational life. If investing is your thing, you could live a hundred lives and never read all the content that is put out every day on the stock, bond, and commodity markets. If food and nutrition is an area that interests you, there are websites that will plan a special menu for you each day. The internet can truly be a new source of vital information and opinions that can help enrich your life. Go for it.

Step 7. Get out your photo album or view the photos on your computer.

When was the last time you looked at your old photographs? There's no point in having them if you don't look at them and remember all the fun you had when you were posing for them. Keep in mind that sometime soon, you'll be feeling that good again. Now is the time to start planning for future events, which will be video or photo-worthy.

It's also a good time to take some selfies of yourself or others in front of different backgrounds, like your home, school, office, favorite store, or wherever you enjoy being—maybe even mowing the lawn or cooking. Some day in the future you'll have a lot of fun saying, "Did I ever look like that?!"

Step 8. The Best Day

A neat way to feel really good for a day is to pick a day that is a few days from now and designate it as "your happy day." You should be looking forward to when it will arrive, and when it finally does, you will do everything in your power to make it indeed "a super happy day."

Lindsey Krause wrote about this in a November 29, 2021, New York Times article in which she pointed out that so often, the days we were expecting to be exciting, like New Year's Eve, are anything but that. However, very often, the days you look back on as having been unusually happy were ordinary days when so many things just happened to go right. Things such as talking to a good friend you hadn't talked to in a while and recalling how much fun the two of you used to have, or listening to a favorite piece of music you hadn't heard recently and had forgotten how much you enjoyed it. These are some of the things you can plan in advance for your own "special happy day."

But don't put it off. Today is a great day to get started, and the most important point to remember when you wake up on that morning is to be determined that on this day, your first and only priority will be to enjoy yourself and do whatever makes you happy! If you like, you can review the sections of this book that give ideas on how to do it.

When your "happy day" is over, you might feel a letdown. Unfortunately, you can't will yourself out of a depression. You can't think yourself out of a gloomy mood. No amount of thinking happy thoughts, mantras, or repeating "I will be happy" is going to do you much good when you're on the verge of tears because of a serious event that turned out badly. What is needed is your deciding to take action to push the blues away. As a Japanese proverb says, "Vision without action is a daydream." So, when we're feeling down, we don't need to ruminate about it but take active steps to counteract it.

I'll discuss many action-oriented steps in Chapter 7 that you can do by yourself.

In Chapter 8, I recommend activities that will re-orient your life toward the outside world and bring people back into your life.

These three approaches in Chapters 6, 7, and 8 combined will reduce your focus on your own unhappiness and help restore your optimism, confidence, and self-worth.

Chapter 7: Do Something by Yourself and for Yourself

Happiness is the only good,
The place to be happy is here,
The time to be happy is now,
The way to be happy is to make others so.

– Robert G. Ingersoll, American Lawyer, Writer (1833 – 1899)

Feeling blue is comparable to your car running out of gas. It's a very simple mechanical problem for your car, and it only requires going to a gas station to remedy the situation. You and your psyche are far more complex. What brings about your bad mood in the first place is also more complex. It is undoubtedly a confluence of many events and thoughts which have gone through your head. Possibly interactions with other people as well.

Whatever the factors were, the net result is that you feel discouraged, disappointed, and lack hope that things will improve. These are the three main ingredients that create depression for normal people. And when they come at the same time, they can cause a situation in which you run out of motivation to do anything.

What happens then? A part of you just gives up. You hit rock bottom. Instead of having energy, enthusiasm, and optimism, you are lacking in each one. You tell yourself, for example, there is no point in looking for a new job, trying to lose weight, or planning a vacation because you will just come up with a dozen reasons why it wouldn't work and can't be done. In your depressed state, the vacation will seem to be too expensive; besides, you can't spare the time; it wouldn't be any fun anyway; you've no one to go with, etc.

I knew a man who owned a liquor store and never took a vacation for over twenty years. According to him, he had to be at the store every minute that it was open. Then he married a woman who managed to convince him that if he took a short vacation, his store wouldn't come to an end because his salesman could wait on the customers without him. And guess what? The store did just as well without him as it had done with him! In his semi-depressed state, he was convinced he always had to be there, but he didn't. So, being depressed can skew your thoughts.

When you are depressed, your brain concludes that whatever you've been doing to turn things around isn't working, and therefore, there is no point in continuing. Your emotions are telling you that you might just as well give up. These feelings sideline you and put you out of action for a while. So, now you need to pivot and take action to get back on track.

Here are some steps that don't require mental focus but physical action on your part.

Step 1. Enjoy little things that can give a big lift to your spirits

Run a bath or turn on the shower. Take a nice warm, calming soak in a tub with a bubble bath and perfumed soap that you may have but rarely treat yourself to. Or take a long, relaxing shower. Clear your mind of other thoughts and just enjoy the feeling of the soothing, warm water. Be focused on this moment because the calm you will feel will help you relax and de-stress.

As you are enjoying yourself, admit that when you are "in the moment," you aren't focusing on your worries. Your mind has pushed them into the background. You've successfully banished your stress and anxiety for this moment. And there are other things you can do that will accomplish the same result like:

- Shine a pair of shoes.
- Polish some silverware.
- Make your bed every morning, so it is tidy and inviting.
- Clean and polish your favorite wood piece of furniture.
- Clean and wax your car.
- Organize a closet.

You will be surprised at the satisfaction you can get from doing some old-fashioned housework or chores. When you've finished, you'll get a very warm feeling from admiring what you've accomplished. Then remind yourself that all the time you focused on that activity and then admired your handiwork, you weren't thinking about your problems. You were in the present, in a positive mood, and accomplishing something satisfying. Bottom line: Your stress and anxiety were reduced, and you felt better!

Step 2. Go for a walk.

This certainly doesn't require a great deal of willpower; in fact, almost all of us walk every day as a means of getting to where we want to go. There is certainly nothing threatening about going for a walk. You don't have to take a long walk or a fast walk, just get outside and walk as long as you like, but for a minimum of just ten minutes. You can do this.

My father lived to be 101, and one of the things which helped him sustain his health and morale was that he always took a walk down to the end of our street and back, which must have been close to a mile. He was proud that he did this every day regardless of the weather, which could be daunting in the cold Vermont winters. His secret was that he always hummed or sang the lively German song "Lili Marlene" out loud as he walked along. Who knows, you might enjoy your walk more if you try humming or singing like my father.

As you take your walk, you will have lots of time to think, and you can think about many different things. The imperative rule concerning your thinking is that you can't ask yourself questions that will require negative answers. The reason for this, as we learned in Chapter 4, is that our brain operates something like a computer.

Ask your brain questions that induce negative replies, and you will get negative replies. Naturally, this will only depress you more. Ask questions that will elicit positive replies, and you will get positive responses which will enable you to start taking positive actions which will make you feel better.

Examples of questions that elicit negative responses are: "Why am I always the only one who isn't having a good time?" and "How come I always end up a failure?" or even "Why can't I find someone to marry?" You may also wonder, "How come I don't have more good friends?" or "Why can't I earn more money?" If you ask yourself negative questions like these, your brain will come up with some good answers, which can seem very logical but can be very wrong. The real trouble with them is that they'll be negative answers.

For example, if you ask yourself why other people seem so much happier than you do, your brain may answer, "They are better looking and have more money than I do." We know that not one of these factors may be correct, but they will make it seem that you can't change your state of unhappiness. These are the kind of negative thoughts that can only increase your unhappiness.

Let's get back to our walking exercise and find out what questions you should ask, which can lead to simple pleasures as you walk.

- What's the most impressive aspect of the sky right now?
- Is the sky covered with puffy clouds like cotton balls?
- Is the sky pure blue or shades of blue?
- Is the sky obscured by light rain or snowfall, and how far ahead can you see?
- If it's nighttime, is the sky black?
- Are there many stars out?
- What shape is the moon?

All these questions are non-threatening and not difficult to answer. They'll take your mind off your own sadness and frustrations and focus it on the outside world instead. One reason that happy people are happy is that they aren't constantly thinking about themselves. Instead, they're focused on other people, events, or surroundings.

An excellent question you could ask yourself as you are walking is, "What's the most enjoyable part of this walk?" The answer could be one thing, or you could surprise yourself and admit that you are enjoying it for several reasons:

- It's great to just get out of the house for a change and away from the TV or whatever aspects of the same old rut you just walked away from.
- You look up and find you are enjoying the beautiful sky.
- Maybe you see other people.
- You haven't gotten any exercise in quite a while, and this walk feels so easy.
- You enjoy seeing interesting buildings, nice homes, tempting store windows.
- If the weather turns bad, it can be an exciting challenge for you just to stay out due to swirling winds, a sudden downpour, or even a heavy snowfall. Whatever the case may be, pay attention to all of it.

When you come home, ask yourself this question: while I was walking and focusing on my surroundings, was I thinking about my problems and feeling unhappy? The answer will probably be no. You were able to successfully focus on non-threatening surroundings and people, and the walk actually reduced your stress and anxiety.

Step 3. Do some form of exercise.

If the weather outside is simply abominable or you don't have time to take a walk, you can do exercises at home on your own. You can do something simple like sitting in a chair and holding a soup can in each hand and raising and lowering your arms from your waist to your shoulders, or even overhead if you can. You could challenge yourself a bit more if your balance is good and try sitting up and down in a chair without using your arms to balance you, thus giving your legs and core stomach muscles a workout. If you have the strength, you can try jumping jacks, touch-your-toes, sit-ups, or pushups.

You could try yoga, tai chi, or floor Pilates. To be sure you are doing the exercises correctly and safely, you can find classes on the internet for every kind of exercise at every level. Those I mentioned above share similar benefits: they help improve strength, balance, and flexibility as well as heart health.

Get on an exercise bike or the real thing outside and enjoy the sun and wind as you go exploring.

Just do as much exercise as you can of whichever type you can manage. The point is that physical exercise will take your mind off whatever is causing you unhappiness. And as important, exercise increases the level of feel-good endorphin hormones that are naturally released during physical activity. Exercise can mean brighter moods and more energy.

Thus, whether it is a walk or some form of more strenuous exercise, these action-oriented activities that you can do by yourself will take your attention away from your problems and lift your spirits. This will have several immediate benefits for you.

- Finishing a walk or exercise will show you that things aren't as hopeless as you may have thought just a few minutes ago. Instead, you have willed yourself to walk or exercise, which shows you that you are in charge of your life. This fact is extremely important and will help raise your self-esteem.

- Exercise is wonderful for your posture and general health.
- Because you are doing something instead of just thinking and feeling sad, you are also getting yourself into the present, which is extremely valuable.

Abraham Maslow is one of the most famous names in American psychology, known primarily for describing the hierarchy of human needs. He also pointed out, "I can feel guilty about the past, apprehensive about the future, but only in the present can I act. The ability to be in the present moment is a major component of mental wellness."

Think of someone who is leading a healthy, active, constructive life. Isn't he or she living in the present? It is the less successful people who spend hours watching television, dreaming of a vacation, thinking of the happy days of their childhood, or just ruminating on how bad their life is and the mistakes they made years ago.

Here is a little poem that can remind us of how important the present is:

Yesterday is history.

Tomorrow is a mystery.

But today is a gift,

And that's why it's called "the present."

Of course, this is basically a clever play on words, but there is also a lot of truth in it. Yesterday is history, and there is very little you can do about it. Tomorrow is a mystery which no one can know, a fact which anyone who has ever tried to predict the stock market, or the weather, knows only too painfully well. Today, however, is a gift, and it is what we've been given in our life, so we better be grateful for it! Take "the present" and say to yourself, "Thank you for today." Or, as my wife likes to say, "Every day above ground is a good day."

Step 4. Get a pen and paper.

Here's a simple thing you can do. Write down the answer to the question, "What did I use to do when I was happy?" For example, your list might include:

- calling up and seeing friends.
- going to a movie.
- making your favorite recipe.
- catching up on some household chores.
- going to the gym.
- taking a vacation.
- going shopping.
- weighing yourself.
- sending out thank you emails/texts or handwritten notes.
- finishing a work project.

Only you know what these things are. Write them down.

Pick the one thing out of all the items on your list that seems the easiest to attempt, even in your sad state. Then write down all the steps you need to accomplish that activity. Then write down the reasons you aren't doing it right now. Weighing the benefits against the negatives, you should be able to decide if it is worthwhile to make an effort.

Additional support and encouragement to translate this exercise into action are provided in Chapter 9, "Bad Habits That Can Rob You of Happiness."

Step 5. Make small, purposeful changes.

If you are intimidated about making changes, you aren't the only one. Many people fear change and the disruption it brings to their routine and their lives, but change is inevitable in life. Nothing in our personal life or business environment stays the same forever. For example, you might find you occasionally eat at a different time than normal, take a different route to the supermarket, or when you order a meal and something different is on the plate, you taste it because it's there. These are all changes. Small changes you make without even realizing it. And these changes mean you are flexible, adaptable, and open to experimenting.

I want you to think small because small changes are the easiest to make. Let's say you are sitting at your desk. You can rearrange the things on your desk. Put the light on the other side, change the laptop from left to right. If you have a landline, you can move the phone from the back of the desk to the front. Try out these changes and see if they make your life function better or not. Maybe you'll find that it's much easier to pick up the phone in its new position. If it makes it harder to use, then you can put it back to where it was originally. This doesn't mean you failed in your choice; it means you learned something. And if you admit you learned something, then you are on the right track and will feel better about experimenting.

Other small, purposeful changes you can make that don't cost anything are:

- Improve the message on your answering machine to be more friendly.
- Rearrange the furniture in a room. You'll be amazed at how many different positions are possible for even a few pieces of furniture and what a difference it can make in the appearance of your home.
- Eat somewhere else in your home occasionally. The kitchen dinner can instead be on the sofa watching TV, in the formal dining room used only for guests, or even in bed. Change for the sake of change is a good thing and means you are flexible.
- Rearrange your magazines. Put all the same magazines together, or file them by date with the newest ones in front. Either way makes them easier to locate quickly.
- Change your schedule in the morning. Would you be more relaxed and happier if you gave yourself ten minutes more time in the morning to get ready? Your body would hardly notice getting ten minutes less sleep, but the extra time you get to shower and dress and perhaps watch a bit of news could cut down on your stress noticeably.
- Watch less TV in the evening and devote the time you save to something that you might find more worthwhile.

After making small changes, you might be ready to make some bigger changes in your life. For example:

- Do a digital detox for one week and turn off all your electronic devices and TV two hours before you go to bed. Make this a family affair so you can talk with your children. Read a book. Have a relaxing, private time with your spouse or partner.
- Stop being a couch potato and buy a gym membership to get in better shape.
- Join a singing group, choir, or glee club and feel a part of a tight-knit family.
- If all you do is work, leave it behind and travel. Expand your cultural horizons, try new foods, de-stress!
- Learn a new skill and sign up for cooking classes. Take what you learned home and practice on family and friends.
- Overcome your fear of public speaking and join Toastmasters. You'll benefit from practice and feedback on how to speak in public.

Making changes, small or big, can have a positive impact on you for three important reasons.

- It shows you that you are in control of at least a part of your life instead of accepting everything the way it is.
- You can accomplish something worthwhile, no matter how small, which can make your life easier, more efficient, or more joyful.
- Change can also be refreshing mentally. A fresh start. A clean slate.

So, don't be afraid to try new things. Think of change as a growing experience that will help restore your confidence to make decisions; boost your morale because the result is worthwhile; and make you more optimistic because change can be enervating and positive.

Step 6. Get something accomplished that you've been afraid to begin.

Maybe it's doing your taxes, paying bills, cleaning up your closet, or returning a phone call. Whatever it is, you know what it is. If it is a big task, like sorting out the books you want to throw away because you don't have any more room on your bookshelf, break it down into discrete parts. One of the best ways to do that is to divide it into time slots. Instead of saying how much time it is going to take to reorganize all the glasses and dishes in your kitchen cabinets, decide that you are just going to get started by working on it for thirty minutes a day. When the thirty minutes are over, be sure to stop! Believe it or not, stopping at your agreed time is just as important as starting in the first place. Why is this?

Because if you keep going, you will get more done now, but the next time that you contemplate working on it for thirty minutes, the memory will come back of the last time when you actually worked for an hour and a half, and you'll decide that you really didn't enjoy it that much and that you don't feel like working for another hour and a half.

So, stop when the time is up. Remember the old show biz adage? Always leave them laughing and asking for more. Better to stop when you are having fun than to push yourself for a longer time when you aren't having fun. You want to come back tomorrow to finish the job, but if your memory is one of having a miserable time, you mightn't do it.

A sister-in-law of mine, Swanee Hunt, was so impressed with a quote from Eleanor Roosevelt that she made a part of it her official motto which is at the bottom of all her stationery and every email. The quote is, "We gain strength and courage, and confidence by each experience in which we really stop to look fear in the face." Mrs. Roosevelt could have said as well, "You must do the thing which you've never been able to begin." Once you manage to take the very first tiny baby step of doing the project, the rest will be that much easier. It is up to you. What are you waiting for?

Step 7. Send someone a card or flowers.

Visit a card store and look at all the cards they have for almost every occasion. They even have cards that say, in effect, I'm sending you a card even though there isn't any special reason to do it. What you say by your action of sending the card is far more important than whatever is written on the card.

What your actions are shouting is that in the midst of your busy life, you thought about the card's recipient in a positive way and that you cared enough about them that you went to the trouble of going into a card store, taking the time to select a card which was appropriate, paying a few dollars to buy the card, and then located a stamp, and their address, and actually mailed the card. That's saying quite a bit.

If the person you are reaching out to is a woman, then you could consider bringing or sending flowers. Many men think of flowers as things that take up space in a room until they wither and must be disposed of. To most women, however, flowers are a symbol of beauty, and the giving of flowers is a token of caring or even of love. You will want to write a note. It doesn't have to be a long message: just 'Thinking of you, from your friend Jack' will often do nicely. Or you can say 'from an admirer' or 'from a secret admirer' and have fun imagining the pleasure and puzzlement that will be going through the mind of your recipient.

Step 8. Buy and maintain a plant.

What's so wonderful about buying and caring for a house plant? How can a plant possibly add to your happiness? Well, not only can it improve your life, there is proof that it will. In an actual demonstration with hospital patients, those who had plants in their rooms got better faster than those who didn't. How can a plant help a sick patient get better? For one thing, a plant is always changing and growing, so it is easy to get hooked on its progress. Is there a new bud? Is the flower still growing? How much bigger is it than it was last week? A plant also needs care and is dependent upon its owner for its continued existence, so these are real reasons why the owner needs to be involved. You can start with a small plant and move on up and have as many as can fit in your home.

Step 9. Get a pet.

In most parts of the US, the people who work with us often become our best friends. But in the competitive atmosphere of much of the financial industry, that's definitely not the case. In fact, on Wall Street, the prevailing ethos is that you eat what you kill, which means that you only get paid for the money that you personally bring in. Being part of a team that does the work is good, but the person who really gets paid well is the one who brought in the business, and when it comes to getting credit for bringing in the business, it is everyone for themselves. This can include a lot of people with very sharp elbows. So, it isn't surprising that when a junior Wall Street banker complained to his boss that he didn't have any friends at the firm, the boss said, "If you want a friend in this business, then get a dog."

The boss made that comment to defend the unfriendly character of the firm, but we can turn it around and utilize it for the very friendly statement he made about the dog. Yes, we do want a friend, and why shouldn't we consider having a dog, cat, or another pet for our friend?

In Dale Carnegie's book "How to Win Friends and Influence People," he points out that almost all animals have to work for their livelihood. In the wild, animals virtually spend their entire life searching for food and at the same time avoiding becoming another animal's dinner. On the domesticated front, sheep grow wool, cows produce milk, chickens lay eggs, and beef cattle produce steaks.

A type of animal that may not produce anything tangible but nevertheless is one of the most popular of them all is those we regard as pets. Many dogs and cats perform valuable services such as acting as watchmen or catching mice, but the real value of most pets today isn't their functionality but the fact that they can create love in their master or mistress, and because of that, we humans need them more than any other animals regardless of what marvelous food or beverage the others can produce. In our society today, cats and dogs are often among the most prized possessions of their owners.

The wonderful thing about having a pet is that no matter what kind of a pet it is, it gets you into caring about another entity. Like many of the steps in this chapter, this does two things for you. It gives you a worthwhile outlet for your positive feelings of caring for another being, and as you become emotionally involved in your pet, it helps to take your feelings of unhappiness away from yourself. It is hard to be unhappy when your pet golden retriever is wagging its tail and looking up at you with joy in his eyes because you've just returned home. It is hard not to be contented when your lovely cat is sitting in your lap and purring away like a miniature sound machine.

But of course, your pet doesn't have to be a Labrador or even a Poodle. Dogs are wonderful and loyal pets, but they can be expensive to maintain and require a lot of your time. Some apartment buildings don't even allow them. If a dog is out of the question, the next choice to consider is a cat. Cats are generally less emotional in their love for their masters than dogs, but they can be very comforting sitting in your lap and purring contentedly.

Then there are a huge variety of other pets. Why not visit a pet store and see for yourself? There are birds, some of which can speak or are ready to be trained by you to speak, there are hamsters, a wide variety of fish from goldfish to big Koi, and the list goes on. If you already know you want a cat or dog, don't forget to look at your local animal shelter, where you will be saving on the purchase price and helping a neglected animal to have the good life it deserves.

It frequently happens that there is a real bonding between the pet's owner and the pet, to the extent that the owner almost feels as if the pet were a member of the family. The owner will have so much affection for the pet that she or he is willing to pay for operations it needs that can cost thousands of dollars. When the pet dies, the owner often goes into a period of grieving, just as if the pet were a relative. But as long as the pet is alive, it gives elation to its owner, and taking care of it gives the owner a sense of purpose. Most importantly, it can provide a deep emotional relationship that gives the owner's life a richness and sense of satisfaction that normally can only be duplicated by one's own family.

Step 10. Plan your next vacation.

Everyone needs activities they can look forward to, and one of the ones that almost everyone looks forward to is a vacation.

It's easy to get ideas of where to go. Many of us probably listen to well-traveled friends. It's also fun to get your own ideas via travel magazines all filled with beautiful color photos of places to go with descriptions of things to do there. And if you go on the internet, you'll be inundated with recommendations on destinations, hotels, restaurants, and sightseeing tours in all price categories.

When you've decided where and when you want to go, research airline and lodging reservations. The internet makes this so easy to do.

It's hard to overestimate the importance of advance planning. I once took a trip to Europe which was planned by a friend of ours. He picked the hotel and what we were going to do each day. He did pick the best sights, including the museums, but somehow nothing worked. We got to the main museum we were going to see that Tuesday and found out, to our surprise, that the museum was closed on Tuesdays. So, we decided to move on to the other museum that we had planned to see that afternoon. We arrived at 11:45 am only to find that on Tuesdays, it was open in the morning and closed at noon!

Here are some of my favorite travel tips:

- If you are flying overseas, remember you probably won't get a full night's sleep on the plane, so don't plan to do something as soon as you get to your hotel.
- What a lot of experienced travelers do is take a two-to-four-hour nap shortly after they arrive. Since hotel rooms aren't generally available until

3:00 pm, you should consider making your hotel reservation starting the day before you plan to arrive and let the hotel know that that's your plan.

- If you're not satisfied with the room you are shown, just go back to the reception desk and tell them politely but firmly that you are disappointed with your room, and ask for a better one at the same price. You will often be successful and may even get an upgrade because the staff wants you to be satisfied and recommend the hotel to your friends.
- There is nothing worse than rushing from one place to another, never really having time to linger and enjoy where you are. So, plan enough time at each site, and check on the internet how long it takes to get from one place to the next, so your schedule doesn't get backed up.
- Allow extra time for meals. We Americans may be used to dropping into a fast-food place at 12:30 and leaving in 15 minutes. However, in Europe, especially France, you can wait at least 15 minutes just between each course!
- If you want to experience high-end restaurants, try doing it at lunch when you can save a bundle compared to what dinner would cost.
- Travel as light as you can. My wife and I each pack for a one-week vacation in a rolling suitcase with four wheels that we take on board with one carry-on bag each. We've learned it's OK to wear the same pants and top several times. Almost all hotels offer overnight laundry service.

- Use a four-wheel, upright rolling suitcase that glides alongside you so easily that you can use just two or three fingers to steer it. Your smaller carry-on bag can balance squarely on top close to the telescoping handle, so you don't have to carry the bag over your arm.
- Using a two-wheeler carry-on bag whose handle pitches the whole suitcase forward puts pressure on your wrist, and you must pull it along through today's mile-long airports!
- The same goes for hauling a heavy duffle bag hooked over your arm or a bulky bag with a strap on your shoulder.

Step 11. Make a List of Some Happy Memories.

I've said many times you can't will yourself into being happy. But it's also true that you can focus your thoughts on any subject you wish, and these thoughts can have a real impact on your mood and feelings.

By making a list of your happy memories, you focus your thoughts on those moments in your life which brought you the most joy. Just writing them down, then slowly reading over each entry, will help you bring back satisfying memories from a happier time. These happy thoughts will fill your mind, banish your blues, and lift your spirits.

One way to get started is to look at the camera roll on your phone or a photo album.

But don't think only of times when you were happy. Try to recall times when you did something for someone else, which you remember made them very happy. That memory of the joy on their face certainly counts as a happy memory for you.

Step 12. Take Up Gardening.

> "One is nearer God's heart in a garden than anywhere else on earth."
>
> ***– From "God's Garden" by Dorothy Frances Gurney, English hymn-writer, (1858 – 1932)***

Whether or not you agree with this famous line, there is no doubt that gardening has a profound positive impact on millions of people around the world. It combines so many of the themes which give us happiness: a chance to create something of beauty; the pleasure of an activity that can have a direct impact on our environment; the challenge of working with a not-always-helpful Mother Nature; the opportunity to do something where we can see rapid and tangible results from our efforts; and finally, a chance to enjoy the great outdoors.

We previously discussed the benefits of taking care of a plant. Well, gardening provides the same benefits multiplied a hundred-fold. Of course, not everyone can have an outdoor garden, such as apartment dwellers like me, but there are several things one can grow indoors using hydroponic plants, orchids, succulents, and air plants. And if you are really lucky, your apartment may have a balcony on which you can plant or keep window ledges on which you can affix window boxes.

You can get started in many ways. If there is a garden supply store or nursery nearby, you can talk to them about the best plants or flowers to use in your locale. The internet can direct you to many books and magazines on gardening and to contact any gardening clubs in your area.

So, if you have the time and place for a garden, I urge you to get started on this project. A garden in and by itself could increase your level of happiness immeasurably. As one commentator noted, "Gardening is cheaper than therapy, and you get tomatoes!"

Step 13. Learn to re-frame events.

There are probably many events in your life when you felt unjustly treated. Every time you dwell on one, you get angry all over again. The result is that it continues to poison your happiness as you imagine how much better your life would have been, had it not happened.

Unfortunately, you can't change what happened. These are historical events that happened in the past and will forever be facts. But what's interesting about facts is that your reaction to them can change dramatically.

You can learn to re-frame an event that has caused you to be unhappy by considering a different interpretation of the same event, which wouldn't have caused you such unhappiness.

Let me tell you four stories that illustrate the point above.

What if you were buying a newspaper in a hurry one morning, and you thought you gave the vendor a dollar bill and then sped off.

Later, when you checked the cash in your wallet, you realized that you must have given him a ten-dollar bill by mistake. So, you lost nine dollars. You might feel stupid and thoroughly upset at yourself for making such a dumb mistake, or you could be angry at the vendor for not having said anything when he must have noticed that you were making a mistake. But no matter how you viewed it, this incident upset you for the rest of the day and maybe longer.

Let's assume that later that day, you have a talk with your accountant about your income taxes. She told you previously that you would receive a refund of $2,324. But in a conversation today, she mentioned that she made a minor error in one of your deductions so that the refund is only going to be $2,224. What's your reaction?

You probably say, "I don't care as long as it comes soon." And yet you've just decreased your net worth by $100, which is eleven times as much as you lost in the morning, and you don't even think about it for a second.

Look at the tremendous differences here in your reaction. With the wrong change, you are furious, perhaps because it was your fault and perhaps because it seems like you lost a huge amount compared to the cost of the paper. The loss of $100 from the tax refund doesn't seem like very much compared to the much larger amount of the refund. Furthermore, there is certainly no way you can blame yourself for the loss, and besides, it really doesn't even feel like a loss since you aren't parting with any money, just receiving a small percent less than you were expecting.

It is only normal that under these circumstances, you would feel vexed about the $9.00 you lost at the newsstand and totally relaxed about the $100 decrease from the IRS.

The same thing happens with other events in our lives, which is to say that the circumstances surrounding an event can completely color it. Here is the second example.

If you happen to see a girl you know walking nearby and you say hello, and she doesn't acknowledge you and just keeps on walking, you say to yourself that you must not have spoken loud enough, and you walk on. But if the same thing happened and the woman was one of the biggest snobs, you know, you would be certain in your mind that the person heard you all right, but just pretended that she didn't because she really didn't want to acknowledge your presence.

Here you've two cases of people who didn't respond when you said "hello." In the first instance, you might mention it to your friend. But in all likelihood, you wouldn't even bother. In the second instance, you are probably telling everyone in your group that this gal is terribly stuck up and that she completely ignored you right on the street when you said hello to her.

Often you don't know the motivations of the other

person, but your interpretation of the event plays a big role in your reaction.

For the third story, we go to the world of money.

Let's say a hard-working person you respect runs a small business. He tells you that while the business is sound, he's temporarily low on cash and would like to borrow a modest amount of money from you at a rate of interest that's acceptable to you. You make the loan.

Later, it turned out his competitors moved their manufacturing overseas and were selling at a price he couldn't match, and he was forced out of business.

He had to sell his premises for a price that barely covered the mortgage and was left with a pile of debts.

He tells you he's very sorry, but he just doesn't have the money to repay you the balance owed. What's your reaction?

When this actually happened to me, I paused, thought of my comfortable circumstances versus his misery, counted my blessings, and told him, "My friend, you did your best. What happened wasn't your fault, and you've suffered far more than I have. Forget the loan, and don't give it another thought." After it was over, I felt good about myself and hoped he could get a decent job where he could continue to support his family. I re-framed how I looked at the event, so instead of feeling angry at myself and cheated, my interpretation made me feel good that I had helped someone far less fortunate than myself.

Now let's take another investment case, where a salesman makes a pitch about a new company planning to compete in China where he has top-level contacts. You invest the same amount of money as you had loaned your friend, but later it turns out that the company was a scam, and the entire investment is gone.

Your reaction would probably be one of outrage. The nerve of anyone stealing money from you! And your rage grows as you think of that lying salesman who duped you.

In both examples, you've lost the same amount of money - and yet your reactions are completely different. If anyone asked why you were so angry in the second example, you would have said it was because you lost a large sum of money. Yet, in the first example, you lost the same amount of money and had no anger. In fact, you felt sympathy and compassion for the person who was responsible for your loss.

The conclusion here is that it wasn't the mere loss of the money which determined your reaction. It was the circumstances around the loss that really determined your emotional reaction. It was your human reaction to the motives and actions of the other person which determined your emotional state.

Here is the last example. If you like someone, you usually like what they do. This can be very clear in politics.

If someone is in your political party and they do something which may not be totally ethical, you tend to say something like, "well, everyone does this, so it is nothing to get excited about." But if a member of the other party does the same thing, you are likely to say, "Those damned (Democrats or Republicans) are always trying to get away with something, and this time those rotten creeps should be prosecuted to the full extent of the law!"

Reframing can definitely apply to human relations. Suppose you are dating someone, and it looks very likely that it is heading into a long-term relationship. Suddenly, the other person says they can't see you anymore, although they assure you that the break-up has nothing to do with you.

You are stunned, confused, and angry. How could they do this to you without any warning or explanation? It's outrageous, etc., etc.

Now let's suppose that you learn that their mother had died and your date had given up all social life to help arrange the funeral and other related matters. Immediately, you feel better. Your anger is transformed into sorrow, and you try to contact them to offer consolation.

What if you had found out that they had actually left you because they were now dating one of your friends? You would be beside yourself with pure rage! Words could not express the intensity of your anger. That disgusting, deceitful person should rot in Hell!

Let's examine what has happened here. In each case, the result is exactly the same, i.e., that your friend is no longer dating you; instead, your friend is dating one of your (former?) friends. Nothing will change those facts.

But we are not so much here concerned with facts as we are with your state of happiness. And look at that gigantic change in your happiness as the facts were reframed.

What if one of your friends becomes cool toward you. Was it because he no longer wanted to be your friend, or was it because he misinterpreted something you said?

These five examples clearly show that you can have completely opposite reactions to a similar set of circumstances when you reframe it. So why not try to re-frame an event that has caused you to be unhappy, and consider if there is a different, more positive interpretation which can make you feel better about the situation. If you can re-frame it and then embrace it, the more positive viewpoint will lift your spirits.

Chapter 8: How to Bring People into Your Life

"Without friends, no one would choose to live, though he had all other goods."

– Aristotle (384 BC – 322 BC)

We, humans, are social creatures, so most of us need frequent social interaction to maintain our equilibrium. In fact, the ability of humans to speak to one another is the primary reason humans have risen to preeminence above all the other creatures on earth. Thus, it's no wonder that speech is such an essential part of our life.

In fact, the more interaction we have with others, the more human we will be, and the more likely that we will be happy. A simple example of this is comparing humans to cats. A cat can be alone by itself all day while its owner is at work, and as far as we can tell, it will be perfectly content. But what was the last time you spent eight or nine hours without any human interaction and enjoyed it? No TV, no cell phone, audiobook, podcast, YouTube, or computer, because watching and listening are interacting. And the great popularity of the previously mentioned activities confirms that many of us, at least partially, are addicted to human interaction. So, how can you come out of your shell when you are feeling really down? You do it via social interaction.

Step 1. Reach out and touch someone

This is a famous advertising line from AT&T a few years ago, and it embodies what you now need to do. The steps in this chapter are action-oriented and bring other people into your life. They aren't difficult or threatening if you do them the right way and contact the right person.

This is an important step because it is so much easier to bring ourselves out of a blue period when you have some interaction with others. Other people are like strong anchors out there in the real world whom we can reach out to and hold on to in order to regain a sense of who we really are. Keep in mind that our friends likely don't think of us as depressed, moody, or negative individuals unless we've told them we feel this way. So, getting back in touch with them can be a positive, reassuring experience.

Whom do you call? It must be someone who will listen to you in a sympathetic manner and who won't be critical. If you have a best friend or supportive parents, those are the people you should call first. Next would be other close friends and your favorite relatives.

Later, when you've built up more confidence, you'll feel like calling more people, and you'll be surprised at how many people there are out there for you to call. When we're blue, it can seem as if we're all alone, and there is no one who cares about us. When we're happy, we feel that we're a kindred spirit to dozens of people who share our values, our interests, and our wellbeing. So, the more people we reach out, to the better it will be for us.

There are many types of people you can get in touch with:

- Someone you haven't talked to in over a month.
- A relative who may be lonely.
- A person from your office whom you talk with a lot in the office but haven't yet talked with outside the office.

- An old classmate.
- A person from your religious group.
- A neighbor.
- Someone who did you a favor, and it doesn't matter how long ago it was; thank them for it, even if you've already thanked them once before. People love to be appreciated.
- Someone you know who now lives a great distance away from you.
- Someone who can answer a question you want to be answered.
- Examples of questions you might want to ask are: What's a good movie playing now? Is there a new restaurant I should try? What vacation suggestions do you've? What's the best new novel you've read? What's the latest gossip about our group? When is the family (or old gang) going to get together again? What are your plans for the holidays? What are you doing this week or weekend?

Once you've made these calls, there is no reason you can't call these same people back. Some you'll want to talk to frequently, others once a month or every few months. But the more you stay in touch, the stronger the relationship becomes and the more benefit you get from it.

Step 2. Call someone with the idea of planning to get together with them.

This is probably the most important idea in this chapter because other people are so important to your having a fulfilling, happy life. Humans are social animals, and while we can certainly enjoy being by ourselves from time to time, there is no doubt most of us have much more fun when we're with others.

Whom do you call, and what should you plan to do? Call your best friend and do what you already have enjoyed doing together.

- Go to the movies.
- Eat at your favorite spot.
- Go shopping.
- Hang out and play video games.
- Enjoy tennis, pickleball, or whatever your favorite sport is.

The important part is that you are taking the initiative. You called the person of your choice and suggested what to do together, instead of waiting passively for the phone to ring. You did what needed to be done to turn the thought into reality.

Studies have shown that the more friends a person has, the happier they're likely to be, the better their health will be, and that they're likely to live longer. So, everything you can do to become linked to more people is a positive step toward your goal of happiness. Calling up someone to arrange to get together is a very important start of what will become a happy and long journey to connect with more and more people.

Step 3. Decide to help someone you know.

How are you going to do that? It all depends upon the person you want to help. The easiest people to help are those who are lonely because you can give them real help just by telephoning them. These people could include an older relative, or perhaps a younger person who has just moved to a new city. Other people you know may be having a difficult time in their lives and would love to hear from you. When calling, you can say that you called because you were thinking about them and wanted to find out what was new, and wish them all the best in the future.

You know which people will be happy to hear from you. These are the people you want to call now. It is important to know why you are doing this. You are doing it because you want to help someone else. You are also doing this because when you do reach out to help someone, it will make you feel better about yourself. And one of the prerequisites of being happy is having a good opinion of yourself. By helping another person, you are directly helping yourself to attain the goal of your own happiness.

Be very clear that you aren't doing this because you want the other person to be grateful to you or to like you more than they do. Not only are these selfish reasons, but neither one of them may happen. With respect to anticipating gratitude, remember that some people don't know how to express gratitude, and sometimes people don't like those who are trying to help them. The basic point is that we can't control other people, and we've no idea of what they'll do when we try to help them. So, it is important that we don't expect gratitude from those we help.

Dale Carnegie had a wonderful story in his all-time best-selling book, still widely available, and titled "How to Win Friends and Influence People." The story is about Andrew Carnegie (no relation), who was probably the richest man in America at the end of the twentieth century and one of our greatest philanthropists. He once decided to make a trip to Ireland to visit the town of his ancestors. There he briefly met and shook hands with some distant cousins.

When he died, it was discovered that he had left a bequest to each of these people whom he had met, which of course, was totally unexpected. Did these distant cousins send a letter of gratitude and name a street after him? Of course not! They instituted a lawsuit claiming that the bequests were too small!

But that doesn't matter. Just as a great person like Andrew Carnegie didn't need any gratitude from his distant cousins, when you do something to help someone, you are doing it for its own sake because of the impact it has on you and not because you will be considered a hero by the recipient. In fact, when you help someone, you should never expect gratitude. That isn't the reason you are doing it. If the recipient of your help expresses gratitude, that should come to you as a wonderful surprise, which would make your good deed even more satisfactory for you.

But if it doesn't happen, that doesn't diminish your good intention or the fact that you went to the trouble to help a person whom you believed needed a personal message, a favor, or a financial helping hand from you.

Some people just have a very difficult time expressing appreciation - but that's their problem and not yours. You are doing this because it is the right thing to do and because it will make you feel better about yourself.

Step 4. Use the internet to make new friends and get back into dating.

We all use the internet daily, but we could be getting a lot more out of it. Are you on Facebook? Millions of people have done so and are enjoying the experience of meeting new internet 'friends.' It's a great way of interacting with others, especially if there are reasons why you can't meet in person.

If you are looking to increase your social life or to get married, you should consider the many dating services available. You might be worried about the malicious characters out there who pretend to be someone they are not, so check out anyone as much as possible. Nevertheless, I have been surprised by how many of my friends and even relatives have been able to find outstanding spouses from these services.

Step 5. Volunteer to do some work for an operating not-for-profit organization.

For purposes of this section, an operating organization is one where they need volunteers to do their work—for example, running a soup kitchen that gives out free meals for those who can't afford them or volunteering to work at a hospital. This is very different from the many major organized charities where the actual work of the organization is done by paid employees, and where the major role of a volunteer, or even a board member, is often simply to give money to the organization and then to ask their friends to give money by coming to various fundraising events. If you have the personality for this, that's great. But for most people, this isn't a lot of fun, and I don't particularly recommend it as a way to attain happiness.

What I am recommending here is doing the work of the organization, which benefits their clients. There are so many of these organizations with such a variety of purposes and clients that you should be able to find one that suits your personal interest and skills no matter where you live. So many religious and other not-for-profit organizations run shelters and soup kitchens for the homeless, including The Salvation Army. And you don't have to work with the homeless if this isn't your choice.

Many museums use volunteers to act as guides and to operate various reception and visitor desks. Most hospitals have volunteer programs which can include delivering mail, reading to patients, or getting meals to them. Nothing can make a person happier than knowing that they've directly helped someone who needed assistance.

There may be organizations in your area that help the elderly. If there are, they probably need volunteers to go shopping for the elderly who are home-bound, just to make a friendly phone call once a day or even just once a week to an elderly shut-in who no longer has any friends or living relatives. Public and private schools often use volunteers to help teachers in the classroom or do one-on-one tutoring for those who need some help with their studies, or assist in sports and other extra-curricular activities. If you want to volunteer, there should be no excuse that you can't find an appropriate organization.

I also recommend working to help those less fortunate than you. The organizations that deal with the poor generally provide soup kitchens and/or run shelters and usually need dozens of volunteers to help serve up the meals, help in the dining area, monitor the shelter, deliver the meals, etc. This is real work, and the people doing it are directly helping those in need. Many volunteers report that this is one of the most rewarding parts of their week. The reason is that here they aren't trying to get something out of an activity, such as money or recognition for their goodness, but are concerned with putting their energy and heart into helping others who need what they're donating.

Even though most of the clients will never become your friends, you may be surprised at how much fun you can have talking with them. Another great insight which you will get is how happy some of the clients are even though they're desperately poor. It proves again that material possessions aren't necessary to lead a life of joy.

Another source of joy from volunteering is that the volunteers often have a lot of fun talking with each other, not in the sense of laughing and telling funny stories, but just in sharing a quiet sense of satisfaction from knowing that they're doing something worthwhile, which has a measurable, visible, positive impact on a number of people who are less fortunate than they are.

One of the secret reasons that charity work is so satisfying is that you aren't only helping others, but at the same time, you are automatically beginning to appreciate how fortunate you are to lead the life you do in comparison to the clients of the organization.

Not everyone has the time or ability to volunteer for a charitable organization, but for everyone else, there is always the opportunity to provide financial support. Obviously, we can't all give billions to a charity like Warren Buffett and Bill Gates have done. But there are plenty of ways we can make a smaller difference by giving to a worthy cause of our choice. Many people are already giving to their own religious organization. It isn't too hard to add other causes, which will greatly appreciate your contributions. Especially as people reach maturity, they often realize that they have enough money to meet their own ongoing financial needs and still have money left over. If you fit into this category, why not give away a significant portion of your wealth while you are alive. It really is true that you can't take it with you.

The solution to this problem is to start giving now to causes you believe in. And there are so many causes in the world which need your help. Start with ones you already have a connection with, such as your college, your political party, or a charity associated with your religious organization. Then think about what really bothers you about the world today and see if you can find a charity that's trying to do something about it. We'll explore donating to charity in more detail in Step 7 below.

There is also a double purpose for you to give to a charity. The obvious point is that your contribution will be used to make this a better world to live in by improving the lives of those who benefit from the charity. But just as important for our purpose and the reason that giving to a charity is included in a book on happiness is that it makes us realize that we're really pretty good human beings who can be very happy about the good things we're doing with our lives. What more can we ask for?

Step 6. Get active in an organization.

You don't have to belong to an organization to have fun in the world, but it certainly can make it a lot easier. Since we humans are naturally social creatures, anything that can bring us together with others who share a mutual purpose will fulfill our basic natural desire to mingle with other people. Other people are so important in our life, and we've been interacting with them for so long that we usually just take them for granted.

Think about the progression of your life. When you started your life, your family was always around you. Then after a few years, you had your class in school which provided you with all the friends and social life you needed. In high school, you had your group of friends and developed special interest groups such as sports teams, the high school band, or debate clubs where you probably made more friends.

If you went to college, you might have joined a fraternity or sorority or used your dorm as your social hub. To a large degree, just being enrolled in a college is being part of an organization that can provide a lot of social contacts. Students also join organizations to accomplish what they want and get experience that can be valuable for the rest of their lives. Examples of organizations that can teach a lot about how the world works and thus be very helpful in later life are student government, school newspaper, ROTC, organizations devoted to influencing others, such as a political club or an organization to support peace or help the homeless.

We celebrate the power of the individual to do wonderful things, but in the real world, it takes an organization to accomplish big tasks. It takes an army to win a war; it takes an active political party to win an election; it takes large corporations to provide the goods and services which we need in our everyday lives.

More importantly, from the happiness point of view, is that belonging to an organization helps us see how we can cooperate with others to bring about a worthwhile goal that's far larger than what any one of us could accomplish by him or herself. Being in an organization also builds interpersonal relations among its participants and enlarges each person's outlook.

In my life, I love playing tennis which gives me contact with my opponent. Playing doubles with a partner is an even better way of cooperating and interacting with another person. I also have enjoyed singing in a group of about ninety men who get together every Thursday evening to rehearse for the two concerts we put on each year in Lincoln Center. It's a great way to get to know a lot of interesting people who all have in common their love of singing in a group. There are many organizations whose primary purpose is to provide human interaction, such as social clubs, fraternities, service organizations, or sports teams. Whatever your interest, get out there and join in. With any organization, the more you put into it, the more you get out of it!

Step 7. Become a Philanthropist.

We tend to think of philanthropists as multi-millionaires or billionaires who give away huge amounts of money to various charities. But there is no minimum dollar amount in the definition of philanthropist. Even on a tight budget, there are plenty of ways you can do good in the world and make a difference by giving to a worthy cause of your choice. Many people are already giving to their own religious organization and perhaps one of their schools, and it isn't too hard to add other causes which you already know that will greatly appreciate your contributions. There are so many people in the world who are suffering and desperately need your help and so many worthy causes that almost everyone can find charities that will appeal particularly to them.

You can make provisions in your will to leave money to various charities, and that's a good opportunity to be generous because you don't have to worry about having enough money for your living expenses once you are gone. Fortunately, some people realize this as they reach maturity and when they still have years of living ahead of themselves.

These people should seriously consider giving away that extra money while they're alive. And giving money for charitable causes you believe in or to loved ones in the next generation should be a source of great joy. So why not get the pleasure of giving while you are alive and can enjoy it. The benefits to you are that you can see the good which you are doing, and you will be able to appreciate the thank-you notes and letters which you receive.

If you are affluent and want to give away large amounts of money, don't be afraid to get all the information you can on the cause to which the charity is giving. If they're any size at all, they'll have people on their staff whose entire job is to encourage people to donate to them and to give out information on what they do. Visit their offices if you can and talk to as many people as are available. Ask questions. Bigger philanthropists aren't shy about asking questions, and you shouldn't be either.

One of the questions philanthropists ask most frequently pertains to the ratio of the cost of raising the money they receive compared to the cost of running the organization. Obviously, you want as little money as possible to be sucked out by the expense of seeking donations and for as much as possible to go to accomplish their mission.

Another question you might want to ask is how active are the members of the board of directors? They're the non-employees most intimately connected with the charity, and if they aren't giving generously themselves, then you might wonder why you should. At a minimum, every member of the board should be donating something every year.

As we said earlier, donating to worthy causes is one of the best ways to immediately feel better about yourself. And feeling good about yourself is practically the definition of happiness!

Step 8. Tell a Joke.

There are risks in almost every human endeavor, and telling a joke is no different. I do it as often as an opportunity arises. However, for too many people, the very idea of taking center stage to reel off a joke is enough to scare them to death.

What if your listener has already heard the joke before? What if you mangle the punch line? What if, when you are halfway through the joke, you forget the punch line? What if when you are finished, no one laughs because they just don't get it? Or they get all right, but they don't think it's funny. Recently after I finished a joke, someone said, "Max, that is the second-worst joke I have ever heard in my life." To which the correct reply is, "I am sorry I disappointed you. Perhaps, you could tell us all a better one?"

Professional comedians will tell you if you tell enough jokes, every one of these bad things will happen to you sooner or later. However, the enjoyment you can get from making other people laugh is so wonderful that you almost can't get that feeling of exhilaration from doing anything else!

Here are the steps to telling a joke. Not one of them is difficult:

- Select a joke. The best source for jokes is the internet and someone who told you a great joke. If you can't remember part of the joke you heard, don't be embarrassed to call the person and ask them to repeat it. They'll be flattered that you liked their joke so much you want to retell it.
- Write it down and make any revisions you need for your audience. For example, "There were these two old men…." can be changed when you're telling it at a girl's school to, "there were these two young gals…."
- Read it out loud when you are alone. As you speak naturally, you automatically raise and lower your voice, and you can do the same thing when telling a joke.
- Read your joke out loud again and again until you can tell it without looking at your note. Remember, a joke is nothing more than a short story.
- Tell it to someone. Pick someone who is non-critical, and just go ahead and tell it as you've successfully done several times to yourself.

If you can update your friends on what happened last night in your favorite TV program or share a description of the final point in a game you watched --then you positively have more than enough memory and narrative skill to tell a joke!

It's been my experience that there is almost nothing in life that requires so little effort and produces such an immediate and pleasurable reaction from others as telling a joke. And if you can make others laugh, then it's almost a certainty you'll get a wonderful sense of joy from it, which will lift your spirits too. Research has found that people laugh five times as often when they're with others as when they're alone.

Step 9. Dance the Night Away

Many people today love to dance to high decibel music and move around the floor free-style without touching their partner. What I'm suggesting you learn are more traditional dances where you need a partner and move around the dance floor as a couple: foxtrot, waltz, rumba, salsa, swing, and even square dancing.

Dancing, like many of the activities on this list, has at least two reasons why it's such a wonderful way to pick up your spirits. First, it's a lot of fun, and second, it's always done with other people so it may be an opportunity to expand your circle of friends or at least to meet some new people with whom you can go to dance parties.

How do you get started? Contact the dance schools in your area. Look on the internet. Give them a call. Many will even give you a free introductory lesson. If you decide to take a series, you might discover you are a good dancer and end up getting very involved in the dance world like a friend of mine did. He and his wife met on the dance floor, clicked as a team, became good friends, and ended up going to amateur competitions all over the country.

Step 10. Give a Party.

This may seem like an ambitious undertaking if you feel blue, but the basics are simple, and the rewards many. A party can be defined as any number of people who get together for the purpose of having a good time. There usually are refreshments and snacks or food served. But those are the only requirements in addition to the people.

There are so many kinds of parties that there is literally no limit to the variety. If you want to start out with a simple party, just tell four or five people that you are getting a group together in a few days to watch a ball game or something else on TV. That counts as a party.

The point is that you are the one making it happen, and you are the one responsible for making it a success. What you need to do is think out in advance what the steps are.

- Decide on the kind of party. Let's say it is watching a ball game. You then must learn the time it will be broadcast and invite your guests to come a bit before.
- Invite the guests, which you can do by whatever is the easiest means of communication, whether it is by phone, in person, texting, or a written invitation.
- Inventory the supplies you need immediately. Do you have enough glasses, plates, napkins, silverware, and seating?
- Buy the party supplies in advance.
- Buy the refreshments in advance.

- Buy or make the snacks and food and have them ready well before the party starts.
- Get any ice you may need to buy a few minutes before the guests are expected.
- Oversee the party. Your job is to ensure that everyone is engaged in conversation, that you introduce any new people to the rest of your guests, and that you don't run out of refreshments.

Obviously, as you get more involved with fancier parties, you will have more to do, such as sending out written invitations, devoting more time and money to the refreshments, and perhaps hiring people to assist in serving, bartending, and cleaning up. But the basic formula remains the same. Bring together a group of people who you believe will be compatible, combine that with a warm and friendly atmosphere, and let everyone enjoy talking with one another.

You will either know everyone at your party or tell your guests to each bring a friend you don't know, so it expands your circle. Hopefully, you'll get a kick out of your role as the host. Many people have a better time being hosts at their own parties than they do when they're attending other peoples' parties.

In addition to having a good time, you should know that you contributed to giving others a good time which is an important contribution you've made. You may also get several people saying "thank you" via a phone call, text, email, or even flowers the next day. You might even be surprised several days later by receiving a handwritten note in the mail. All these forms of thanks and praise will be well deserved and should lift your spirits.

Lastly, if you think a good reason to give a party is that the people you invited will invite you to their parties in the future, you may be sadly disappointed. Usually, not everyone can reciprocate, or they may just not want to invite you. Unfortunately, you can't count on anyone reciprocating, so this isn't a good reason to give a party. The real reason for giving a party is because you expect to have a wonderful time talking with your friends and new acquaintances in a happy environment, giving them a good time and enjoying yourself.

Step 11. Can you increase the enjoyment you receive from your sexuality?

The reason that this step is in the form of a question is that not everyone has a sex life, including children, the very elderly, people who aren't in a sexual relationship, and those who refrain from sex for religious or moral reasons. This section obviously isn't for them.

But for those millions who do have a sex life, it's interesting that some married couples take it for granted without giving it any thought as to how this aspect of one's life can be improved. Professional sex therapists are adamant that sex should be a major source of enjoyment in most people's lives, and if it isn't a big source of satisfaction in yours, then there are steps you can take that might improve it.

Sex therapy is an entire world of its own, with literally hundreds of books and articles written on the subject. A book on happiness isn't the place to present the entire subject. What I can point out is that if you believe you aren't getting the amount of enjoyment you should get from your sex life, there are definite things you can do to improve it.

You could start with a book on sex therapy, which could be quite helpful. I suggest "She Comes First." By Ian Kerner. It's every man's must-read. The author offers what some men think is a radical new philosophy for pleasuring a woman: oral sex. It's not foreplay. It's core play. Learn other tried-and-true techniques for consistently satisfying a woman. Then for women is the author's second book, "He Comes Next." In this point-by-point guide, the author covers every angle of male sexuality and the secrets to his satisfaction.

Consulting a professional therapist is another obvious choice. Most practicing psychologists and psychiatrists can be helpful here, and there are some who specialize in sexual therapy.

Sex is often not an easy subject to bring up because it is so personal, and almost anything you say to a spouse or partner can be interpreted as criticism. But, if you don't discuss it at all, the likelihood is that the problem will linger and fester for years. So, if the choice is to risk having your loved one think you are being critical or not having a good sex life, then the choice is clear. Get up your courage, pick the right time and place to discuss it, and then plunge in.

If your spouse or partner loves you, they'll be willing to listen to what you've to say. You might start the conversation by saying, "Please don't think that what I'm about to say is in any way a criticism of you. This isn't a question of who is at fault or of casting blame. I'm simply seeking a means of having a better sex life for both of us. So here is my thought..." Just because it isn't easy to discuss sex in an objective way, that doesn't mean that you shouldn't try.

Almost every reason people give for having poor sex lives can be improved upon if the two partners will just sit down and give it some thought. As an example, a young couple with little children will often feel that they don't have any time alone when they can enjoy sex. So, they need to create a time when they can. Children do have to sleep, and once they do, there should be an opportunity to lock the bedroom door and have some privacy.

What about men who say they just don't have any interest in sex anymore? We've all seen advertisements for drugs that can assist men in having sexual arousal. Unfortunately, if the man isn't interested in having sex with his partner, there is no point in taking the drugs. But if the problem is that while he wants to have sex, he just can't get an erection, then drugs, such as Cialis, Viagra, and Levitra, may be effective.

If there is still a problem, you can turn to your primary care physician for some pointers and for a referral to a specialist in this subject.

Step 12. Express your gratitude.

It is so much easier to get yourself out of a blue period by having some interaction with others. The interaction can be in person, at a distance by phone, text, email, or a note. One important way to bring people back into your life is to express your gratitude to them. Tell the people who have done important things for you, even in the distant past, that you appreciated their advice, loyalty, sacrifice, financial help, moral support, time spent with you, and gifts. Expressing your thanks not just once but a second time later will make the person who helped you feel deeply appreciated, and you'll be rewarded with their thanks for remembering. Thus, the interactions you will have with these people will be a win-win.

So, make a list of the people you should contact and what they did for you. Remind yourself that they feel you are worthy of their interest, concern, affection, monetary support, and time. This truth will boost your morale and lift your spirits.

You can also express appreciation for ordinary things that happen to you. For example:

- A store cashier gives you a welcoming smile.
- Your mailman never fails to say "hello" when he sees you.
- Your server starts your meal with a cheerful greeting.
- A taxi driver jumps out and gets your packages from the trunk for you without you asking.
- A little league coach takes extra time to work with your son on his batting.

- One of your relatives calls you for no other reason than just to see how you're doing today.
- A teacher gives a more detailed explanation of something which you hadn't been able to understand.

Let me end this section with a true story about the value of simply saying "thank you." Nick, the son of a friend of mine, worked in a very upscale restaurant and told us a story about the owner who had a string of successful restaurants in Boston. The one aspect of service the owner was unbending on was that whenever anyone did something for someone else, that person had to say, "thank you."

Not just to customers, and not just for things that happened in the dining room, but even for little things that happened in the kitchen where no one was present besides the people involved. So, if the person scrubbing the pots and pans handed you a fork, you had to say, "Thank you." Nick told me he was amazed at how this small sign of appreciation and respect fostered goodwill, cooperation, better teamwork, and higher morale among the staff.

Chapter 9: Preconditions That Block Your Happiness

The Precondition of every true calling must be . . .love for mankind.

– Romain Rolland, French dramatist, (1866 – 1944)

Preconditions are the absolute minimum requirements that you believe you must have to be happy. For example, an ambitious college student may tell herself that she cannot be happy until she has an "A" in each of her courses. A single man has decided that he needs a girlfriend who must be: (1) Blond, (2) Over 5" 7" tall, (3) Weighing less than 130 pounds; (4) 32 years old or less, and (5) has a great career which (6) doesn't require her to work longer than 9:00 to 5:00, five days a week. He may actually have a few more requirements than this, but you get the picture. If you asked him why he thinks these requirements are so important, he might not be able to give a good reason, but that is his dream girl, and either he gets someone who meets these requirements, or he will stay single.

This is a great example of the foolishness of preconditions because it should be obvious that if he starts seeing a girl whom he really likes and with whom he has a lot in common, but she is 5' 5" tall and weighs 136 pounds, should he keep on seeing her? Obviously, he should. You can easily see how ridiculous this example is, but the same reasoning can be applied to many other preconditions which people place on their happiness, including those which can seem quite logical to the people who possess them. It's important to understand how these preconditions work because they can be dangerous to your happiness.

They can be dangerous because if you firmly believe that you can't be happy unless you achieve a precondition, then that can become a self-fulfilling prophecy.

Indeed, it can happen that you won't be happy unless you achieve that precondition. The reason, however, will not be that you need to achieve the precondition to be happy, but only that it becomes true because you believe it to be true!

Since all preconditions are just judgments that we have reached, and since many of them may not be possible to attain, it would be a shame to let them rob us of our well-deserved happiness.

Preconditions are one of the biggest reasons why so many of us aren't happy. Preconditions have two effects on us. First, they depress us because we know that we do not have whatever the precondition is, and second, we are fully committed to the idea that until we have achieved this precondition, we are not going to let ourselves be happy. In the earlier chapter on behavior patterns that rob us of happiness, we found it was worthwhile to look at what positive results people got out of their negative patterns.

If we do the same analysis here, we find that the positive effects can be twofold: 1. Having these preconditions to happiness can be a huge motivating force for us. An ambitious businessman who says he will not be truly happy until he can afford to buy a new BMW760Li Sedan could actually be saying to himself that he believes he will be able to afford one within a very few years, and this dream of the BMW is a motivating force which keeps him working so hard. 2. It can absolve him from taking responsibility for his current state of unhappiness.

The single man with the precise requirements for his girlfriend may be unhappy because he doesn't have a girlfriend, but he can easily explain that away by saying he just hasn't been able to find a woman who meets his requirements. He may know many lovely women who would make wonderful girlfriends if he didn't have these requirements, which are not relevant to the success of a long-term relationship. But these absurd preconditions enable him to shift his problem away from himself and the real reasons that have prevented him from getting married. Instead, he can place the blame on all the women he has met who did not come up to his preconditions.

Ironically, while this kind of precondition sharply limits our ability to be happy, it is also our way of saying that we believe we are so special that we should be able to attain these conditions. This explains what is so contradictory about those who are working like slaves to get ahead in their careers and already are making a lot of money. They still aren't happy because there is one more rung they must climb before they have reached their goal or one more digit they must put on their net worth before they have decided that they are a success.

They know that they are stressed out, tense, and unhappy, but they believe these symptoms are an integral part of seeking to achieve their preconditions of happiness. They are greatly surprised when they come across someone from a much lower social-economic level who has not even come close to meeting their preconditions but is nevertheless quite happy. It could be a cab driver, a household domestic, or a worker in the grocery store.

The point is that these workers have not put a condition on their happiness. They are happy in their present lives, right now.

The striver has said to herself that she can't be happy until she has a net worth of one million dollars. Of course, nothing could be further from the truth. The thought that you need a certain amount of money to be happy is one of the silliest notions that exist. Study after study shows that rich people are only slightly happier than poor people, and this slight difference could easily be explained by the fact that people with money can afford better health care.

The advertising industry certainly deserves some of the blame for the fact that so many people believe that if you are not spending a lot of money on an activity, it isn't really being done at its best level. You may drive out to the country for a picnic and have a wonderful time. On the way, someone sees another family driving an expensive SUV. Do you really think that the value of your car has any impact whatsoever on how much fun your family will have? Even if it is a "pre-owned" economy class car with worn seat covers and scratches around the fenders, does that have any intrinsic impact on the enjoyment of the people inside that car?

The view of the wonderful outdoors is the same from either one, as is the time it will take to get there and the music on the radio. Only if you have been brainwashed by advertising will you believe that you can't really enjoy a picnic unless you are going in a Land Rover Range Rover that costs a minimum of $92,000.

Here are examples of preconditions that people create during various stages of their lives to make themselves seem superior to what they believe they really are and to relieve them of being responsible for their unhappiness:

I can't be happy unless:

In college:

- I'm on Dean's List.
- I'm dating a person who is in the XYZ fraternity/sorority, or on a varsity team, or a cheerleader, etc.
- Until my parents believe that I am one of the best students in my class.
- Until I'm accepted at the grad school, which is my first choice.

Into their career:

- Until I'm earning at least $120,000 a year.
- Until I have a full-time assistant just for myself.
- Unless it looks like I am on track to get a promotion.

Mid-Life

- Until I become at least a VP.
- Until Iget a bigger home in a better neighborhood.
- Until I get my kids into good colleges
- Until I have at least $2,000,000 saved up for my retirement.
- Until I can take at least a three-week

vacation every year.

- Until I get better at my golf, tennis, dancing, bowling, gardening, French, cooking, etc.
- Until I lose 6 pounds or get to the gym four times a week.
- Until I get accepted into the _____ (fill in the blank) club, group, social society, etc.

Older Years:

- Until all my children call me at least once a week
- Unless I can take three cruises a year on a luxury cruise liner.
- Unless my retirement income increases to at least 30% above what it would be if I retired now.

As an example of how foolish these conditions are, I am reminded of the shoeshine man where I spent twenty years of my life working as a stockbroker for Bear Stearns in New York City. For much of that time, I was in a large boardroom with about thirty other brokers. Most of us were pretty ambitious, and we spent a large part of our time figuring out how we could increase the income from our existing clients and even more time trying to get new clients. It wasn't always fun when the potential client didn't agree with us on what was a good investment, and it was often filled with disappointments when a stock that we had fervently recommended went down instead up. As someone put it, it was "A tough way to make an easy buck."

One day, as I looked around at all the people in that boardroom, I was struck by an amazing insight. I was looking out at all the brokers struggling to make more money and realized that most of them were not particularly happy. I also looked at their assistants, who earned substantially less than the brokers. They were all chatting with one another and seemed, if anything, to be significantly happier than the brokers.

As I was looking around the room, I saw the shoeshine man who came around each day to ask if anyone wanted a shine. He was an immigrant who had four children and had somehow managed to get all of them through college. He was always cheerful. It occurred to me that he was both the lowest paid person in the room and the happiest one by far. He wasn't saying, "I can't be happy until I'm making over $250,000 a year," like so many of the people in that room. He was leading an almost ideal life in all the ways that counted.

How easy it would have been for him to be miserable, surrounded as he was all day long by men and women who were earning many, many times what he was. In addition, they were on the phone all day long doing a job which to him might have seemed a lot more fun than shining shoes. He could have asked himself, "Where did I go wrong? Other people have immigrated to the U.S. and become millionaires while I'm still doing this lowly job with no chance of advancement?" However, instead of asking that question, he reveled in thinking of what he had accomplished. I believe he was the happiest person in the room.

He was having a wonderful time because he didn't put any preconditions on his happiness. Instead, he was working as hard as he could at the job which he had. He had a worthwhile goal, which was to support his family and to put his children through college, and that's what he had accomplished. By having a realistic goal with no fanciful preconditions, he was able to become an example of a happy person.

His story shows the foolishness of preconditions on happiness. There are no preconditions other than what we create for ourselves. If the conditions we set for our happiness are realistic, then that is the normal condition of human life. After all, everyone should have goals that they are striving to attain. Even if you are retired or are a trust fund beneficiary, you still must have goals for leading your life. It isn't the idea of goals that causes unhappiness; it is the superficial and arbitrary goals that are unrelated to our real needs that cause the problems.

Let's go back to the man at the beginning of this chapter who had so many preconditions about his future wife. Almost any happily married person will immediately point out that his preconditions have nothing to do with having a happy marriage. How many people tell the divorce judge, "Your honor, I am seeking a divorce because I discovered that my wife is not 5 feet 5 inches tall but is only 5 feet 3 inches tall."

That may have been a precondition to his marriage, but I guarantee that no one ever wanted a divorce because of that. The real reasons for divorce are far more substantial, like finding out that your spouse has completely different values from you, or isn't in love with you anymore, or is in love with someone else.

Everyone should have some qualities that they are looking for in a spouse, such as do they have similar values to mine? Do we share the same concept of our future lives together? Is she or he supportive of me? Are they kind and loving? Do we have a lot of fun when we are together? These are the important conditions we should be seeking. Unfortunately, some people don't pay enough attention to these important core values while they over concentrate on factors that have little correlation to the success of a marriage. They may later regret it.

The same thing is true of too many preconditions to our happiness. Give it some thought and find out if, even without knowing it, you have some preconditions to happiness in your life that are unnecessarily blocking you from attaining the joy you deserve.

Chapter 10: Behavior Patterns That Rob You of Happiness

"The test of one's behavior pattern is its relationship to society, its relationship to work, and its relationship to sex."

– Alfred Adler, Austrian M.D., a colleague of Freud, founder of Individual Psychology. (1870 – 1937)

Before we plunge into our search for happiness, it makes sense to first find out if we have some specific bad habits which are causing problems in our lives. These problems can be blatant or obscure, although they will have a tremendous impact on your mental psyche. The sooner we address them, the better we can cope with life's challenges and learn to become happy in any situation. If we can lick these difficulties, it will make us that much happier and remove obstacles that can make complete happiness impossible to attain. Here are some such habits with suggestions on how to get rid of them.

Procrastination

Probably everyone is guilty of procrastination from time to time. It can extend from as insignificant an event as telling yourself you will pay the bills tomorrow evening instead of tonight, because you decided that you would rather watch TV this evening, to a much more serious problem such as putting off studying for an exam which you know is essential for your future career. The more important the task you are avoiding, the greater your excuse must be to defeat you from doing it now.

The real dangers of procrastination are that it can negatively affect your life because so many important things that you should be doing will never get done. Also, and even more significant from our point of view, is that you will be going through your life with an enormous and ever-growing list of "to do's!" Your feeling of inadequacy from having failed to do so many things which you know you should have done will depress you and most likely make you feel guilty about failing to do them.

Additionally, you will never feel that you really deserve to have a good time or take a vacation because you know that you should be doing all the things which you have postponed in the past. The dangers of procrastination are real, and they can be serious. Now the question is, how do we avoid these dangers by ending our procrastination?

The good news is that there are several techniques that can work successfully to end or diminish your procrastination. We noted earlier that we can't fool our brain by saying and endlessly repeating, "From now on, I will do everything on time" because we are too smart to believe that. But by the same token, our brain is smart enough to recognize thoughts that do ring true. We start with a big advantage, namely that our brain really would like to be able to do things when they should be done. That is a huge plus. But something is holding us back. If we can diagnose what is holding us back, we can start making progress in curing the problem.

Why do we delay doing certain things? Is it simply because we don't like to do them? Or is it that we are afraid of doing them because of our fear that we won't do them well or that doing them will be very disagreeable. For example, fear of failure is a common reason why students do not study enough. It is because they are under pressure to get good grades so they can move up to the next level, and they're afraid that maybe they won't be able to do it. If this is what they are thinking, then it isn't going to be any fun studying for the exam. Instead of studying more and having a better shot at getting a good grade, they postpone studying, which shortens the time they have to study and decreases their chance of getting a good grade.

Let's assume there is something you just c want to do. Maybe you have decided that you need tc someone something which you know they don't want to hear, such as telling your current significant other that you really think you should stop seeing each other. There are many reasons why this conversation could be very unpleasant for you, so it is completely understandable why you would not want to do it. But on the other hand, if you want to move ahead with your social life, this is something which you feel you must do.

Here is what you can do to make it happen. You can think through what is likely to happen when you do break the news. Once you start to visualize what the other person's reaction will be, you can then make plans to make your announcement in the least unpleasant manner. How do you break the news? What if they say they can't believe you? Or they get angry? Or accuse you of having led them on and wasted their time? Or do they say that they are deeply disappointed in you? Or just tell you to go to hell or worse?

There are thousands of ways the conversation could turn out, and you probably won't be able to predict them all. But just going through this exercise will help prepare you for what is likely to happen. Then you should think of what the worst possible outcomes could be. In this case, maybe the other person will say they will never talk to you again in your life, or that they will tell all your friends and relatives what a despicable person you are, etc.

Say to yourself, what if they do? Your friends will certainly rally to your side and probably will tell you what a creep he/she was to involve them in your private life. And what if your soon-to-be-ex doesn't talk to you ever again? The world is not going to end. There are very likely thousands of people in this country who could fill in for the one you are dismissing.

So, practice what you are going to say, anticipate what could happen, and then decide whether it is worth doing. If the benefit to your being free from this other person outweighs the potential unpleasantness of the conversation, then you will decide to do it. Now, here's the 64-million-dollar question.

How do you actually get up the courage to do it? Here is my suggestion. Pick out the time and place which will be easiest for you, and then tell yourself that you will be much better off once the task is over. You intend to do this at some point in time anyhow, so it might just as well be now because the sooner you do it, the sooner the unpleasantness will be behind you and the more time you will have to enjoy the results.

Make it easy for yourself by doing as much preparation as possible. In this example, you might want to write down the exact words you will use so that when the time comes, all you must do is read them. You might decide that the easiest way to break the news is on the phone instead of in person. You then decide upon the exact time to do it. Let's say you pick this coming Tuesday at 8:30 PM. Next, you decide that you should call from your bedroom. One technique is to set an alarm clock to go off at the appointed time. As soon as it does, you immediately turn it off, and before you even have time to think, you call the number with your notes in front of you.

You have decided in advance what to do if the person does not answer, but instead, you hear a voice mail message. This is your plan B, which can be either:

1. Hang up and call back in 20 minutes,
2. Leave a voice mail for the other person to call you, or
3. Leave a message of what you were going to say.

The point is that you now have a workable plan which considers all the possible outcomes you can think of. You must pull the trigger the second the alarm goes off. It may not be easy but remember that you are well prepared for whatever happens. Just close your eyes, say here goes, and make the call. Think of what a relief and joy it will be when the call is over.

If you are procrastinating about studying for a big exam, you can use some of the same basic techniques. Set an exact time when you will start studying. Pick the place. Incidentally, many people find that it is easier to study when there are others around you who are already studying. Consider going to a study room or library rather than studying in private.

Finally, a helpful technique is to give yourself a strict time limit on when to stop. You may be so thrilled that you finally began studying that you are tempted to keep on doing it until well after midnight. That might be great, but I have discovered that this can make it much more difficult to start in again the next night. Better to leave with a feeling that you could have gone on longer and, in fact, wanted to go on longer. Maybe there's an analogy here to some restaurants which believe that they should always end a meal before their customers feel overstuffed. Be sure to set a stop time and then follow it.

For bigger projects, the technique is to split the task into smaller units and then treat each one as a watertight compartment. If you are working on a Ph. D. thesis, you obviously can't just sit down and write it from start to finish in one sitting. But even smaller projects like reports of all kinds of business assignments can be broken down this way. If you are supposed to call 40 major prospects in the next two weeks, you could do this by calling four people a day. But what if you really don't want to do it because you are afraid that not one of the 40 people will be interested in buying what you are selling, and they'll all give you the brush-off?

How do you push yourself to get started? You get started by using a schedule. The first call should be as soon as possible after you get to the office. Preferably immediately after you take off your coat and even before you have your first cup of coffee. The reason for this is that it's much easier to do something if you haven't already had a chance to postpone doing it. Immediately upon reaching the office, you make the first call.

Then as soon as that is completed, you use the momentum from the first call to energize yourself into making the second call without a break. Then you can relax and enjoy yourself. Be sure to give yourself this time off. This is very important. No one should be under constant pressure to perform. We need our time off. If you push yourself too hard and try to make all four calls consecutively, it may be so stressful that it discourages you from making any calls the next day.

Set a goal and don't do more than the goal. Knowing that as soon as you reach your goal, you can relax for the rest of the day is one of the things that makes it easier to do. If you violate this rule, then you have made it that much harder to accomplish your goal and to enjoy your day.

The same thing is true for projects where you can't divide the task so easily. For example, if you are assigned to read an 800-page book, you can say that you will read some number like 50 pages at each session, or you can say that you will spend a certain amount of time reading, such as one hour. Either way can work. And they are both much better than saying that you will keep reading until you lose interest or get tired of reading.

Procrastination is a perfectly natural phenomenon. We all try to void unpleasant activities, and one of the most common ways of doing this is to put them off until tomorrow. This can be the best approach to a problem if you are tired, surprised by what has happened, or are in an emotional state. A serious problem arises when you know that the very best time to tackle that problem is right now, and yet you don't do it.

You suddenly remember something else which you could be doing like phoning a friend, attending to a household chore, reading the newspaper, or getting something to eat. All these activities make sense to do, but not when they can easily wait and when the real purpose of doing them is to prevent you from doing the important thing which you should be doing right now.

Follow the rules above or visualize yourself doing it now, then think of what the worst result would be you tried and failed. Then compare that with the benefits of doing it now. Then plan out doing it in detail. Set the exact time you will start; prepare everything you will need, such as getting your computer ready if that's what you will use for writing out notes. If it is a timed activity, then decide when you will stop, and it can help to set your timer or alarm to go off at that time. Your first "anti-procrastination" activity may be difficult to accomplish, but once you do it, you will experience a vibrant feeling of success which will make it that much easier to overcome the next temptation to procrastinate.

Fear

This is a normal human reaction that is very useful under the right circumstances. What it does for you is to suddenly send a surge of alertness and energy through your body by speeding up your heartbeat. It was one of the keys to survival for the cavemen who were under almost constant danger from man-killing predators. But today, when the man-eating lions are safely dozing in zoos, fear can be a big liability. If your fear is about delivering an oral report to your management, then it is not helpful to have your heart pounding with dread over what may happen. Furthermore, fear can reduce your ability to think clearly, and it is a very unpleasant sensation that can destroy your happiness.

There is no point in telling yourself not to be afraid. As we've noted many times before, your brain is too smart to believe you when you say there is nothing to fear. If that were true, then why are you afraid? So, saying that you will not be afraid is not going to work. But your brain can understand a factually stated argument. In our current example, your brain may be afraid of your speaking engagement because it knows that you have given very few if any speeches before, and therefore, there is no memory of your having given a successful speech.

Furthermore, you may not have all the facts at your command which you need to properly cover the subject. Or, what if one-third of the way through the speech, you suddenly forget what you were supposed to say next? Finally, you may not have given any thought to the organization of the speech. What part of your speech do you start with? Have you already figured that out, or are you just going to wing it once you get up behind the podium and hope that everything falls into place?

The way to vanquish fear, in this case, is simple. You must take action to demonstrate to your brain that there is nothing to fear because you have already solved the potential problems with your thorough preparation. This preparation makes a note of all the things which you are afraid can go wrong and then sets out to make sure that they will not happen. First, you begin with an outline of what you want to say, organizing your thoughts in a logical manner.

Let's say your topic is how your company can increase sales of its top-of-the-line widget. The first topic might be a description of the extra benefits which this product delivers. The second could be showing the customers why it is worth far more than the additional cost over your regular product. Third could be a comparison with your leading competitors' products in the same price bracket showing specifically where yours is better. If you are a distributor, a final major point could be a discussion of the best means for getting the first three points out to the customers, listing the pros and cons of personal visits, phone calls, emails, or sending salespeople out to industry conferences.

There should always be a conclusion in which you summarize the main points you have made and conclude that because of these points, it should be possible to increase sales of your top-of-the-line widget by X%. Now, you have solved one of the reasons for your fear, namely that you won't know what to say when you stand up to speak.

You still haven't deleted all the reasons you could be afraid of because you still haven't ever given the talk successfully. So, you decide to give the talk out loud in an empty room. Once you have done this, you might notice some rough patches, and you can rewrite them. Then get a voice recorder and give the speech again. It takes a certain amount of courage to do that and then to be willing to listen to yourself, but it will be well worth it.

Now, you can tell your brain that the talk is going to be a success for the simple reason that you have already given it successfully several times, and making the actual presentation will just be a repeat of what you have already done. Your brain will accept the logic of your thinking, and your fear will subside.

You may not be able to eliminate fear, but don't worry because that is not the real problem. The real problem arises when the fear stops you from doing something or at least doing it well. As every war story points out, fear is something that happens to just about everyone in battle, but that doesn't stop them from fighting. The point is that you can still go ahead and do things even if you are afraid. Soldiers in battle are afraid of getting killed, and they should be because their comrades are being shot every day.

Yet, they still charge the enemy when they are ordered to do so. If you have read and implemented the first part of this chapter, then you know that, unlike the combat soldiers, you have very little to fear. So even if you still have vestiges of fear, just go ahead, and do what you are prepared to do despite that groundless fear you have. When you know that you really have nothing to fear, and you act despite your fear, you will find that the fear will very quickly disappear.

Stress

You've undoubtedly heard that heart attacks are the number one killer in the U.S and that stress is one of the big reasons for heart failure. Stress is also one of the biggest reasons that many people can't be happy. In our modern, fast-moving, and competitive society, there are many situations that are naturally stressful. They tend to be those situations where the outcome is very important to us, but where we have only limited control over that outcome. These situations are very common in sales positions where the customer can have a hundred reasons for not doing something that the salesperson wants.

Stress can also be prevalent in investment management. For instance, a stockbroker may believe that a certain bank that pays a good dividend and is selling at a low valuation is an excellent conservative investment. But her client wants to buy an internet stock. The broker persuades the client to buy the bank stock because it is a more solid investment. Unfortunately, due to market action at the end of the month, the bank stock is down 5%, and the internet stock has gone up 30%. The client decides to get a new broker and closes her account. There are many other examples of factors beyond one's control that can have a large effect on one's future.

Think about any athletic coach. Not only is the outcome of a game not under the control of the individual players, but the coaches are even one level less in control because they aren't playing the game themselves. So, they have to hope that their players will remember all the pointers they have given them. Even if they were in the game themselves, the great unknown is how well the other team is going to play. How many coaches get fired at the end of every season because their players didn't do what the coaches had told them to do? Or their opponents developed a secret new strategy, which they couldn't prepare for?

Gambling can also be a source of stress because no one can control or predict the outcome of the throw of the dice or which card will be dealt. But strangely, many gamblers don't seem to suffer very much stress, and in fact, they get a secret thrill out of it because they think of it as a way to make a lot of quick money, whereas they really should be concerned with the likelihood of losing a lot of money quickly.

The way to overcome stress is to stare the situation in the face and say to yourself that even when you are doing the very best you can, there are certain situations in which you can't control the outcome. That is simply a fact of life, and what it means is that you should be ready to accept the consequences of whatever happens. Any athlete going into a game realizes that she is going to try her very utmost to win, but she still does not know whether she is going to be successful or not.

Some athletes are under terrific stress for fear that they might lose. The better athletes seem to remain calm. I remember one finalist in a major tennis tournament who had just lost, and he was being interviewed by the inevitable TV announcer who asked him, "How does it feel to know that you have just lost the most important game of your life?" To which the player coolly replied, "Don't worry. It's not the end of the world. After all, no one died because I lost."

That's the attitude that can conquer stress. Yes, it is very important to win, and you are going to try as hard as you possibly can to win, but this doesn't mean that you must experience stress. Just remember, half of all athletes are going to lose every game (unless you're talking about golf, where approximately 97% of the players in a tournament don't win). Remember that no one expects you to be a God, and if you tried your best, there is no reason why you should suffer anxiety. Even in circumstances that are much more important than most athletic events, you don't have to suffer from stress.

The classic real-life example of stress is when two people are vying to move up into one position in a company. Each one is trying their very best to be the winner, and neither one knows what the outcome will be. The principle is the same. Accept the fact that you might be the loser and start making some realistic plans about how you would react and what your plans would be at that point. You are not going to die, you're not going to be beaten or fired, your life will go on, and it's up to you to make the most of it at that point. As Marie Curie pointed out, "Nothing in life is to be feared. It is only to be understood."

Perfectionism

This occurs when a person is never satisfied with anything they do because it always falls short of what they expect of themselves. This is a form of conceitedness because the subliminal message is that they are so wonderful that they, among all human beings, should be able to accomplish things that are superhuman. A totally different form of perfectionism occurs when we overly practice it on other people so that nothing they do meets with our approval. This is a great way to alienate your friends because it is actually just a form of unwarranted criticism.

Are you a perfectionist without knowing it? One way to tell is if you are spending more time and energy doing something than other people are doing. Every woman wants to look as good as she can, but if her friends spend about 15 minutes putting on their makeup, and they are spending half an hour, they could be a perfectionist. If even after that half an hour she is still not really satisfied, she probably is a perfectionist. The danger is that she will never be happy because she is living in an imperfect world, where perfection is often not even needed. As the saying goes, "Don't let perfection get in the way of the good."

It has been said that the violin was perfected in northern Italy about 300 years ago by Antonio Stradivari and others and that since then, no one has been able to make a violin as good as those. I have also heard that a regular sewing needle is the absolute perfect shape for its purpose. That's two perfect objects out of the billion or so which exist on this earth, so the odds that you will be able to perfect anything are virtually zero.

Don't keep trying. The way to overcome perfectionism is to recognize that we live in an imperfect world, and so our goal should not be to be perfect but to do things as well as we can, and then recognize that that is as good as it's going to get. Accept that fact and stop being so hard on yourself. Let it go and move on.

Inferiority Complex

It means just what it says, namely that the person suffering from it believes that they are inferior to others on a very basic level. This can apply to virtually every area of their lives, such as how much other people respect them, how well they are doing on the job, and how successful they are. People who have an inferiority complex underestimate their own worth, deprecate their abilities, are not able to see the importance they have to others, and completely miss the value that they are bringing to the world.

An inferiority complex can be extremely harmful because negative thoughts can dramatically hold us back from reaching our potential. A rightfully famous aphorism by Henry Ford is "Whether you think you can do something or think that you can't do it, you will probably be right." And if you're not sure whether you can do something, you'll probably "try" to do it, which means making a halfhearted effort and seeing what happens. The answer is usually a disappointment.

A challenging task is rarely ever completed successfully by "trying" because the very word means that one will "attempt" to do something, which contains the implicit meaning that there is a good chance the attempt will fail. Almost everything worth doing turns out to have unexpected difficulties, and if you are only trying to find out whether you can do something, rather than going ahead and doing it, the likelihood is that you are not going to succeed. That is the very nature of life in the real world. The only way to succeed is to believe that you can do something and then keep trying until you do succeed.

If you constantly believe that you really are not as good as the other people in your department at the office, you will not believe you can compete with them. If that is the case, you're probably not going to try very hard to compete because instinctively, you will not put forth a futile effort. If you "know" that you are not going to succeed, then subconsciously, you are not going to be trying as hard as if you know that you are eventually going to triumph and all you need to do is to apply a little more effort to make it a reality. To succeed, you need to develop the attitude that nothing is going to stop you, and the more difficult something becomes, the harder you are going to work at it.

Even in non-business, non-competitive situations, an inferiority complex can ruin everything. Let's say a normal person meets someone whom they really like. They are saying to themselves, "I have so much fun being with this person that we are probably going to have a great future together." The person with an inferiority complex says to themself, "This person is so wonderful that there is no reason why they would be interested in someone like me." And so, they imagine that the relationship can't possibly work out even though the other person may be very interested in them.

Inferiority complexes can arise from a huge variety of reasons, and some therapists like to take time to explore what originally caused them to arise. But the important point going forward is not how they started but why they persist. Why does this person still believe that they are not as good as most people when it is years after the inferiority complex began? And despite much evidence that they are as competent and as good as anyone else — and better than many others in various areas, why does it persist? There must be a reason for the persistence of this complex. Once we can understand what the reason is, we can begin to work on abolishing it.

The benefit that an inferiority complex gives is that it provides a defense against disappointments. Since a person with an inferiority complex doesn't expect much, if anything, from themselves, they don't try to do things that they fear may result in failures. Since their expectations are low, they don't really expect that they can make anything turn out the way they would like. Therefore, they rarely fail at anything, but they also don't succeed at many things which they could because they don't think they would succeed.

Additionally, it may play into their relationships with others. When they express their doubts and fears about themselves to their friends, the others will rightly point out that they are much better than they think, and their friends will tell them that they are sure to be a success if they just try. This is the kind of reassurance and motivation that they are getting from their complex.

These are the positive results people get from their inferiority complex, and it is undoubtedly why so many people are walking around with them. But the real story is that even the minor benefits which people may obtain from inferiority complexes are not worth one-tenth of what they lose by having one.

Having an inferiority complex can condemn you to fail to live up to your potential because you will never believe that you can do what you are capable of. In addition, you will tend to believe that others are able to do so many things much better than you that you will not even try to do the same things they are doing. It takes so much joy out of life because instead of looking forward to tomorrow, people with inferiority complexes worry incessantly that they are going to fail tomorrow because of their lack of ability or other qualities.

Now that we've seen how damaging an inferiority complex can be, let's see how we can minimize it or even completely eradicate it. We will use the method we used on the other conditions which rob us of our happiness, and that is to give our brain rational and true reasons why the complex is not an accurate description of what and who we really are.

One of the first and easiest things you can do is to give proper emphasis to the compliments you receive. You may not think that you receive many compliments, but it is also very likely that you just dismiss them as being meaningless. Many people who have inferiority complexes are so convinced that they are unworthy that they just assume any compliments they receive must only be motivated by false flattery.

My experience is that most people don't go around giving out meaningless compliments. So instead of dismissing compliments by saying to yourself, "I really don't know whether they meant that or were just trying to get on my good side," give yourself the benefit of the doubt and take credit for what they are complimenting you on.

If someone tells you that you did a good job talking to a dissatisfied client, why not give yourself a little personal celebration? Exult in the fact that someone gave you a compliment. Even if you don't think that it was really deserved because anyone could have done it, apparently the person who gave you the compliment didn't agree with you, or they would never have had said anything.

But they did when they didn't have to. That and the fact that they did should show you that perhaps your opinion of what you have done is too low and that at least one other person believes that you really did a wonderful job of handling that client. If you keep a journal or make notes on your calendar, why not write down the details of every compliment you receive. You may be getting more than you think, and you should be paying more attention to the ones you are getting.

When I was trying to find a publisher for my first book about trading options, I was rejected by twenty-four publishers, one after another. Of course, this was discouraging, and I could have said to myself, "I guess I'm just not made to be an author," and given up. Well, one of the rejection letters said that although that publisher had already decided on all the books for the coming season, they felt that my book was publishable.

I grabbed on to this minor comment like the pilot of an out-of-control plane grabs onto a parachute. I had no idea who wrote that comment, whether they had the power to decide what books they published or not, and whether they really believed it was publishable. After all, they had already said that they could not publish it, so they didn't risk anything by telling me my book was publishable, but taking that comment to heart gave me the motivation to keep on sending it out to more publishers. Eventually, there was not only one but two publishers who wanted to bring it out and were eager to do so.

The next step is to start looking at who you are and what you can do to objectively assess yourself. This is not easy, but if something in your life is measured in an objective manner, then it is a bit easier. If you are a student and you are getting a B in most of your courses, you may think that you are really a failure because you have an older sibling who went to the same school and consistently received nothing but "A's." No matter how well you do, you compare yourself to your sibling and come up short. You say to yourself, "I'll never be as good as he or she was; I'm just not any good at schoolwork."

But for all we know, your sibling could be a near-genius who has better grades than 99.5% of the people in your school. You are unwittingly taking an abnormally talented person as your benchmark of what being a good student should be. It could be that at your school, a solid B is considered a very good mark indeed. Your B may not show that you are a poor student incapable of learning but rather only that your sibling is a one-in-a-thousand gifted student, which you probably already knew. Instead of concluding that you are the family dunce, the correct conclusion is that you are a good student in every sense of the word with a near-genius for a sibling.

The basic antidotes for an inferiority complex are to recognize your good qualities and stop comparing yourself to others who you believe are superior to you. Look at some of the wonderful things you have done and recognize your accomplishments. Are you the most successful in your high school? How about in the top half of your college classmates? Have you raised wonderful children? Have you been a loving spouse? Have you ever given up? Look, you're already reading this book which means that you believe you have a chance to become happy, which is already a step in the right direction. It demonstrates that you have the attitude that you are going to do what it takes to demolish the unhappiness in your life.

Self-Pity

Let's look at the psychology of feeling sorry for yourself. It's so easy to feel that way! You may start out by saying to yourself that you never get a break in your rotten company because they don't appreciate all you've done for them. There is no reason to specify here all the disappointing and plain awful things that have happened to you, but you believe that you have had been made to suffer more than almost anyone else.

Feeling sorry for oneself has destroyed so many lives which could have been happy. Self-pity is hard to fight because there are always many reasons why we could say, "Poor me." It could go back to when you were four years old, and you said, "My brother got a new sled for Christmas, and all I got was this lousy baseball glove." It seemed unfair to you then, and this same reasoning can go on for a lifetime. For example, "Yes, I got a bonus this year at work, but my brother-in-law got a real promotion to become a V. P. while I'm still working at my same old miserable job."

When you look at the world this way, you can always find a million reasons why you should feel sorry for yourself. One could devote an entire book to the reasons, but we'll limit ourselves here to save time. Here is a mere tiny fraction of the reasons why people feel sorry for themselves: I don't have as fancy a car as my neighbor. I never have a winner when I go to the track. Why do I always get a cold every winter? How come we never get invited out to dinner? How come Jack was elected the President of our club, and I'm still just a member of the hospitality committee? Why don't my kids ever get on the honor roll? And how come Paul's son is on the varsity football team while my son can't even get onto the JV team? Why don't my recipes ever turn out the way they're supposed to? How come my life is so boring? How come I'm always a loser?

Of course, we could go on forever. What should be clear by now is that no more awful things have happened to you than have happened to many other people. It's not that your life is so much worse than other people's lives; it is simply how you look at it. By looking at everything that could be better and saying, "Poor me. I have to suffer through this lousy luck I have." A person I knew was interviewing for a job. On the day of the interview, it rained cats and dogs, and the person said, "It's just my usual bad luck that it had to rain on the exact day when I have my interview." It never occurred to them that it also rained on everyone else. It is easy for those who have inferiority complexes to convince themselves that everything in their life is really bad and that their problems are far worse than other people's. The truth is that there are millions of other people in this world who have a much harder and more difficult life than they have, and they don't feel sorry for themselves. So why should they or you?

What is happening here is that they are cherry-picking the examples to which they compare themselves with others and are deliberately picking the ones where they come out second best. But they could just as well pick examples where they came out on top.

Did you get through another year without cancer or Covid-19 and all its variants? If you said yes, that is wonderful news and makes you one of the luckiest people in the world, compared to 100,000's other people who were not so fortunate. So, instead of bemoaning the fact that you didn't get the promotion last year, you could be saying that you were very fortunate to be able to keep your job and even get a raise. Why don't you compare yourself to the millions of people who lost their jobs or their businesses in the last few years?

Once again, the answer can be found by asking what it is that you are getting from your feeling of self-pity. The answer could be that it gives you an excuse to not live up to what you may consider your potential. Let's say you believe that you would be an excellent Vice President in your firm, and it really hurt you when Ted was made a VP instead of you.

You could have taken a rational review of what happened and asked yourself what you could do in the coming year to make yourself more likely to be appointed a VP. Why did Ted get the appointment? Was he outperforming you at his present job? Did he have ideas of how things could be improved? Did other employees seem to like him and ask him for help on what they were doing?

By asking these questions, you could come up with a plan of what you could do this year to be a better candidate next year. But it would be difficult because you might have to admit that you weren't as good at certain things as you would like to have been and that, based on your review, Ted really was more entitled to the promotion than you were. This type of response to his promotion makes it much more likely that you will be the next one who is named a VP.

Let's look at the psychology of feeling sorry for yourself. It's so easy to do! You start out by saying to yourself that you never get a break in this rotten company. They just don't appreciate what you've been doing. Maybe this is true, but by generalizing with a reason that doesn't make sense, like "They're never going to promote me," you get yourself off the hook. You are not responsible for not having gotten the promotion, and the blame can shift to the selfish, bigoted, stupid, etc., management who picked Ted. The result is that you no longer must feel bad about missing out on the promotion.

But look what also happens. You now lock in the belief that, for some reason, you will never get ahead at your company. This, of course, immediately translates into you not doing as well as you can because there is no use in doing well if they are never going to promote you. So, you just go along doing what is required by the job and nothing more. You may be sure that if management had any doubts about whether they should have made you a VP, those doubts quickly vanished when they saw the type of work you are doing this year.

Here is a choice. Take what seems to be the easy road out, which relieves you of the uncomfortable idea that maybe you didn't deserve the promotion. Unfortunately, this leaves you doing the same quality of work you have been doing, which may not get you the promotion next year. Or you can face up to the difficult realization that you could have done better and that if you try harder this coming year, you will have a better probability of being appointed a VP next year. It's your choice.

Compulsions

Among the common compulsions afflicting people are alcoholism, compulsive eating, using narcotics, being habitually late, being a workaholic (which doesn't just mean that you worked long hours, but that you stay in the office excessively in order to avoid problems which you have in other areas of your life), compulsively watching porno on the internet, excessively watching sports on TV or the internet, and having a gambling addiction.

These may sound like very different problems which have to be resolved by different strategies. But the way I look at them, they are all similar in that they are all habits which can be destructive to your lifestyle, and which involve doing something which you know you shouldn't be doing, but which you do because it brings you certain other benefits, even if they are minor in comparison to what you lose. These compulsions are very similar in the amount of damage which they can do to your life.

Perhaps compulsive narcotics, drinking, and gambling are the worst because they can destroy a person's entire life. Others, such as watching TV sports or porno excessively, just consume enormous amounts of time, but that too can have a very negative effect on one's life. At the least, these compulsions are ways to avoid responsibility for things that we find disturbing. When a person is suffering from one of these compulsions, they don't have the time or the ability to think about what they need to be thinking about.

Is there a problem with their marriage? Well, never mind, I'll be able to deal with it better once I've had a couple of drinks, and then I can think about it. Am I getting behind in paying my bills? That's OK because I'm going to the casino this weekend, and this time, I feel confident that it's my turn to really win big. So, it's not difficult to see what people get out of these obviously self-destroying habits. All these compulsions provide a distraction or an excuse to not focus on their problems. These diversions can provide relief from their misery for a short period of time, but they are making their problems much, much worse.

The price people pay for these distractions or temporary highs is that the compulsions can wreak permanent damage on their lives from which they may never be able to recover. Broken marriages resulting from these compulsions can often never be mended. Huge sums of money that are lost to gambling can require years of difficult budgeting to repay debts or force a person into bankruptcy. Either of these can make it almost impossible to ever attain the same lifestyle the person had before the compulsion took them to financial ruin.

How does one end these compulsions? Fortunately, not all compulsions are as total as some of the examples we've given here. A person who likes to have a gin martini straight up at the end of a bad day at the office is not suffering from a compulsion, nor is someone who gets a thrill from risking a pre-determined amount in Las Vegas a couple of times a year. For people who can still function but find a minor case of a compulsion interfering with their total ability to achieve what they want, the answer is to consider the pros and cons of the compulsion.

It may become clear that whatever temporary benefits the compulsion offers are more than offset by the problems they create. So, the first thing you must do is conclude that it is important to your well-being to end this compulsion and that you will do everything in your power to end it even knowing that doing so will deprive you of a certain pleasure which the compulsion gives you. Once you make this commitment and recognize that it is going to cost you some enjoyment, the next step is to make sure that temptation does not creep back into your life and drag you back.

A good way to do this is to ramp up the other aspects of your life so that you will not even have the time and energy to indulge in your compulsion or have any interest in doing so.

Don't overlook the great amount of help available to people who suffer from serious compulsions like alcoholism and narcotics. The best-known source for alcoholics is certainly AA which stands for Alcoholics Anonymous. The name came from the fact that years ago, when it was founded, many alcoholics desperately tried to hide the fact that they were alcoholics and therefore didn't want anyone to know that they were attending an organization that was set up for them. It has been around since 1935 and boasts many successful transformations.

Its basic premise is that the only way to stop drinking is by total withdrawal from the very beginning. They make a point of saying that even one sip of an alcoholic drink could, and often will, be the start of backsliding into alcoholism once again. Their meetings are designed to encourage and give support to those who are struggling with this major change in their lives. One of the reasons for their success is that almost everyone at their meetings has been through many of the same problems themselves and can give motivation to the newcomers by relating how they made it into a world of abstention. AA has now broadened its scope to include treatment for drug abusers as well. It has groups in hundreds of locations in the U.S., and they are very welcoming of potential members. To find your nearest location, go to www.aa.org.

Fear of success

At first glance, it may seem strange to fear the very thing which almost everyone is seeking. Yet fear of success is pervasive in our society. One example of it is in sports. It often happens in tennis tournaments, for example, that an unknown player will be up against one of the top-seeded players in an early round. The challenger is having an excellent day and is fearless in her attack on the famous champion. She wins the first set and then amazingly takes the lead in the second set. Then in the second set, which would determine the outcome of the match if the underdog won, she suddenly starts doing everything wrong. She hits into the net, can't get any speed on her serves, and if she does, the serves go out.

What suddenly happened to turn the game around? Probably two things occurred. One important consideration is that the famous tennis star initially figured this would be an easy win, and she was not playing her hardest for the first part of the second set. Then she suddenly realizes that this match is no joke and that if she doesn't start playing much better very soon, she will be the laughing stock of the tennis world. She suddenly puts on the power which has made her a champion and starts winning.

But another reason for the change in scores has to do with the mental state of the unknown who came into the match fearless because she knew she had nothing to lose. Everyone expected her to lose, and even if she does, she can tell people for the rest of her life how she once played one of the top players in the world. So, she is relaxed and playing her very best. But after she has won the first set and is leading at the beginning of the second set, she can't escape the fact that she is beating one of the world's tennis greats.

This hits her like the proverbial ton of bricks, and immediately she starts thinking that she has a chance to beat this tennis champion. Then right after that realization comes the frightening thought that she could still lose. Now her confidence and fearlessness begin to disappear. It is because of her initial success that she is now in a position where she has something to fear, namely the thought that after she has done so well, the champion will win in the end. And once she starts on that line of thought, she can't do anything right. Fear of success has produced the exact opposite of success.

It is not really fear of success that creates problems but that the thought of it brings with it fear of losing that success. And if you never achieve that success, you will never have to worry about losing it. That's what causes some people to fear success.

The answer to many of these problems is to overcome the fear and to think of the positive results which could be possible. The best way to do that is with an honest look at each situation. Analyze what could go wrong and how bad would it be. Then face up to it by:

1. Recognizing that if the worst happened, it would not be the end of your world, even though it might require some major changes, and
2. Realizing that the probability of the worst happening is quite small based upon your previous experience.

Once you have done this and accepted this worst scenario, your fear will automatically begin to subside. You are now ready to move on and focus on how you can improve your chances for a good outcome.

Chapter 11: Getting Serious About Your Life

"The person without a purpose is like a ship without a rudder."

– Thomas Carlyle, Scottish historian, philosopher, mathematician, and teacher. (1795 – 1881)

This is a book about happiness and having fun, so what in the world is a chapter on seriousness doing in it? Why can't we just live the life of the idle rich, going from one vacation to another all over the world, never having to do any work or anything we didn't want to do, and ending up being sublimely happy? These questions and many others are probably encircling your mind right now, and you want a definitive answer.

Well, there are two answers to these questions. The first practical answer, of course, is that most of us can't afford it. However, the second and far more important answer is that it simply doesn't work. Thanks to the rising wealth of many people throughout the world, there are actually hundreds of thousands of people who can afford to live that kind of life, and many of them are doing just that. And you know what?

After a few years or less of this life, they are frequently no happier than they were before. In fact, they may be much less happy than they were because they assume that they ought to be supremely happy now that they can have a life of leisure. However, in reality, they are not exceptionally happy, and so they feel cheated. They believed that by just doing nothing except "enjoying themselves," they would be happy. And now that they're not, they feel doubly disappointed.

Instead of feeling joyful and filled with enthusiasm, they tend to get bored with whatever they're doing. Let's assume that they love to travel. They want to traverse the world and learn about different cultures and environments. They invest so much into this leisure activity because they know that their inner void will be fulfilled in the long haul. However, after a while, they have seen all the exotic travel locations, and one place is beginning to look like another. Or, more importantly, they just don't care anymore about looking at yet another destination. What's missing from their lives?

It turns out that to be truly happy, you need a reason for your life other than just being happy. As we have pointed out many times in this book, you can't try to be content by just saying that you will be happy. You can't decide that you will fall in love with someone or fall out of love. Pleasure and happiness are two different concepts, and more pleasure does not lead to true happiness. A hungry person gets tremendous pleasure out of a good meal, but if immediately afterward she tries to repeat the experience with another meal, it's not going to produce the same satisfaction.

We human beings have a built-in need to believe that we are doing something outside of ourselves that is validating our lives. In primitive societies, the purpose of human life was authentic and easy to understand. It was frequently as simple as how to survive. The men might be employed in hunting for food and protecting their families from the ever-present deadly attacks of other humans and animals. The women would be working to procreate, raise the children, and provide a domestic life. It was a harsh existence with little time for reflection, but each person knew their purpose in that society. They knew what they needed to do to improve their lives. This was no easy task, but they made it through both their collective and individual efforts. As far as we know, no one thought about it because it was the very essence of their lives.

From almost the very beginning of our civilizations, as the world's standard of living began to rise and people had time to think about the big questions of life, one of the first sources of answers was religion. People needed something that gave them purpose in their lives, and what better source than religion. And while the primary purpose of religion is devotion to God, it can also provide a serious drive to one's life here on earth.

Devotion to God requires attending religious services and allocating time to prayer, and most religions contain rules on how to live a good religious life, such as the Bible's admonition to "love thy neighbor as thyself." The fact that almost every civilization has had some form of religion that contains principles giving people a purpose in life shows the importance of having a life with a purpose.

Today we can create a life without a purpose, and to people who are overworked, over-stressed, and pushed to do more in a day than anyone possibly could do, even with multitasking, it must seem that having all day to relax would be the key to happiness. That is the logical conclusion because, in most cases, people hardly get the time to lay back and enjoy their existence. This is very similar to a person who doesn't have much money, thinking that the key to happiness is wealth. Little do they know that some of the wealthiest people are among the meanest, most jealous, envious, and unhappy people in the world! This has become apparent to virtually everyone who has thought about leading a happy life.

Albert Einstein was even more biting in his criticism of the "feel good" philosophy. He notes that "I have never looked upon ease and happiness as ends in themselves — this critical basis I call the ideal of the pigsty." He continued that the ideals that have motivated his life and have given him new courage to face life cheerfully have been kindness, beauty, and truth.

Many great thinkers have thought about the purpose of life and have come to different conclusions. However, they all seem to agree that there must be some sense of purpose to have a fully satisfactory life. Arnold Schwarzenegger said, "You've got to have a purpose no matter what you can do in life." No less a theologian than Buddha himself said, "Your purpose in life is to find your purpose and give your whole heart and soul to it."

To have a purpose in life doesn't mean that you need a deep and important goal, such as saving the world from the possibility of World War III. However, it does mean that you have some purpose you are trying to accomplish. No matter what this goal is, it will give you a way to measure how well you are succeeding at it and a way to determine what progress you are making in moving toward it. It will also give you a feeling of competence as you begin to approach your goal.

Many people's goals are personal to them, such as to become the best grandfather ever, break the local high school's one-mile track record, lose ten more pounds, or lower their golf handicap by 10 points. Any goal is better than none, though there is a hierarchy in goals. If people want to achieve the best results, they should not only recognize their goals but also establish a detailed and extensive hierarchy placing the more worthy ones at the top.

Purpose in life is such an important aspect of happiness that one commentator has divided the attainment of happiness into two parts: the first part is getting pleasure, and the second part, which can be equally as important, is fulfilling a feeling of purpose. In his book, *Happiness by Design*, Paul Dolan says that any activity can be divided into these two components. For example, watching TV may rank very high in getting pleasure and quite low on purpose, while doing housework tends to be very low in getting pleasure and high in attaining satisfaction from a sense of purpose.

The concept that everything we do can be divided into two parts can be very helpful when you are doing something that you don't enjoy. And we all know that we have several activities which we don't like but which we must do. Suppose you are doing something that you don't like; it means that you are not getting immediate pleasure out of it. And yet, you are doing it. Why is that?

You are doing it because the result of not doing it would be worse than the pain you feel from doing it. You are taking responsibility for your actions and don't want to let your family, peers, colleagues, and even society down. Moreover, your mind tells you that you will be better off by doing it, and it is then that your sense of purpose kicks in and compels you to do the task. Tell yourself that while you may not get any pleasure out of the task, that fact is being offset by a large amount of purpose fulfillment you are getting out of it.

In other words, the very fact that you are doing it shows that you have decided that the sense of purpose you get out of doing it is more worthwhile than not doing it. It shows that you believe the accomplishment of the purpose will more than offset the displeasure of the moment.

Professional athletes give us a compelling example of what a sense of purpose can accomplish. Just consider the determination that any great sports star must have to excel in his or her game. On television, you usually see the stars in their moment of glory, smiling, as the world applauds and the TV cameras roll. The world is their oyster, and they are sitting on top of it.

Yet how often do you see them doing the long hours of back-breaking exercises such as push-ups, running distances, lifting weights, and practicing strategies again and again? These practice sessions can leave them exhausted, sore, and perhaps even injured. However, the athletes continue to do them because their sense of purpose to win drives them far more than their aches and pains, which are pushing them back to take a break.

In fact, the training they must go through is so difficult that it has created the phrase “No pain, no gain.” It’s not just athletes who have to endure difficulties, but almost anyone who expects to succeed in any occupation.

Adversities and challenges are part of life, and the sooner people realize this, the more efficient they will become in every aspect of their lives.

Perhaps the most extreme example is the medical profession. In order to become a doctor, one must first graduate from college, which requires four years of study. Then they must go to medical school another four years. Then they must intern for at least one year, and if they want to have a specialty, they must train for at least another year. None of this is easy, and much of it requires almost sleepless nights plus much memorization.

However, becoming an M.D. is one of the most sought-after occupations in the U. S. Why is that? Because so many people are willing to spend many of the best years of their lives devoted to doing something with a very low level of pleasure but with an extremely high level of purpose. Thank goodness we have people in our society who are willing to postpone their pleasure in the present in order to achieve a worthy purpose in the future.

Chapter 12:
Other People

"Other people" are by far the most important factor in our lives. These very people are the source of comfort, humor, support, relaxing conversation, and, best of all, love. How we interact with others is the style of our relationships, and this style is a key component of our happiness. Study after study has shown that the more relationships people have, the happier they are. One of the basic principles of humans is that we are social animals. We need other people in our lives if we are to be real people. Denying these relationships, we wither away.

If the principle behind most of your relationships is how you can get other people to do what you want them to do for you, then the chances are that you aren't going to have relationships that refresh and reward you. If, however, your basic idea is that you try to do as much as you can for your friends and associates, then they, in turn, will try to do the same for you. These relationships, as a result, will give you long-lasting joy.

A typical problem of many unhappy people is that they believe no one does anything for them. While this may be true, the person is looking at the situation backward. Of course, no one does anything for them because they aren't doing anything for anyone else in their state of unhappiness. If you are a baby, you can be certain that people will do all kinds of things for you, but that's because a baby is both very cute and incapable of doing things for itself.

Now you are an adult, and you do have the power to do things for yourself and other people. So do it; don't worry if you feel you are the one to make all the calls. That's fine. You have the power.

There is almost always some friction between people in a relationship. Marriage can provide one example. People can date for years, but only after they get married, do they realize that some of the personal habits of their spouse are beginning to get on their nerves.

One of the little but classic examples is how to squeeze the toothpaste tube. If you've never been married, you might wonder how there can be different ways to squeeze a toothpaste tube, and if there are different ways, then what difference can it make? But believe me, there are different ways to squeeze a toothpaste tube, and it makes a big difference in how the tube looks afterward.

Some people squeeze it in the middle while others carefully start at the end of the tube and roll it up as they move toward the cap. If you are used to one way, you may not like the other regardless of which of the two ways you do it. As trivial as this sounds, professional marital counselors will tell you that it can create considerable frustration and even anger among newly marrieds.

In a business relationship, other people expect certain things from you. Let's say you have an unreasonable boss who expects too much from all his employees. Very often, there are many different things a boss expects, and if you analyze them, you will find some are very hard and some easy. Do your best on the hard things, but make sure that you really ace the easy ones. In real life, many people don't keep an accurate score. One good deed can cancel out a bad deed even if the deeds are unequal.

For example, say you are in sales. Your boss wants you to increase your sales by 20% over last year and submit expenses for the previous week by the following Wednesday. In this very simplified example, we have two different things he or she's looking for. One is very hard; you spend all day trying to make sales, contacting potential customers, following up with existing customers to get more business out of them, getting referrals, setting up appointments, making presentations, following up the presentations, etc. Still, it's very hard to convince people that they really need to buy your product, especially with all the competition. So, that takes 98% of your effort.

The other 2% is spent on administrative tasks, including the expense report. And of course, everyone is always late with their reports because that's what you do when you have some free time, and since you are so busy selling, there never seems to be any free time to write a stupid report which you don't even get paid to do.

So, here's the point: why not make getting the expense report in early an important part of your job? What if you got your report in every Monday? Do you think the boss would notice? If he doesn't seem to, then you should certainly say something to him. And do you know what? Even if he gets paid on how much the salespeople under him produce and even if you only get paid on how much you sell and getting the reports in on Monday doesn't help you sell one more unit, it still could easily make your boss happy with you. He could point you out as an example, and just the fact that he may like you more could be a great advantage. Think of all the little things he can do for you if he wants to.

And even though getting the report in early is a little thing, it will show your boss that you really do care about your job. You never know when his appreciation could be very important to you. What if there is a slowdown in business and headquarters orders him to lay off 10% of the salespeople. You could be in that group, and if he remembers that you are conscientious on your reports, he may bump you up above someone who is scheduled to be let go.

One of the biggest problems people have with other people is their belief that other people aren't as nice or caring about them as they should be. Many mothers of grown children who are now living on their own complain that their children don't call them as often as they would like. Wives complain that their husbands don't love and respect them as much as they should. Husbands can get depressed over the fact that their wives don't appreciate how hard they must work to pay for maintaining the entire household, and they may feel, especially after the children leave home, that the wives have an easy life. Many employees complain that their bosses don't appreciate all that they do for the company. And what child doesn't rebel against a parent or two from time to time for being totally lacking in understanding of the problems they face every day.

This is closely related to believing that you aren't getting your fair share of rewards in life. We work so hard and long, yet we know that we earn far less than others who put in fewer hours a week and have a lot more fun at working than we do. Even in nonprofit organizations, the same problem arises; it's termed envy. Let's face the fact that, of course, some people in this world don't have to work as hard as we do, but get paid a lot more. The only way that could not be true would be if everyone in the world worked exactly as hard as everyone else, and they all got paid the same amount.

There are natural differences in the real world of capitalism, where people get paid what they can earn on their own or what they're worth to others. But the point is that this is the way it is, and we must accept that fact. The real problem is that we resent it. Maybe there are reasons. A person was born into a wealthy family and now works at the family business. Does he work hard? Perhaps not. But if you are going to resent this, you are going to be one unhappy person. There are many other injustices in this world. What about a woman who happens to have been born supremely beautiful? She gets almost everything she wants in life without much effort. Are you jealous? It could be that the one thing she doesn't have is anything close to happiness.

Another person may have a real natural talent. She can be very creative and, in fact, her boss thinks that she's a superwoman. Instead of being jealous, what can we change about our lives to make us as successful as she is? With this line of thinking, we will no longer be envious of others but actually benefit from them by using them as role models who can help us make our lives more enjoyable.

Then work on our attitude. As long as we have enough for our needs, why should we make ourselves unhappy because someone else has a life that in some ways may appear to be better than ours? The right attitude you should have is one where you can say, "Good for them; I hope they continue to succeed. Meanwhile, I'm having a great time with my life because I'm utilizing my talents to the best of my ability." In a tennis club, I can tell you that the guys and gals playing in the "B" tournaments have just as much fun as those playing with the "A" players. While this is only an amateur sport, it's an example of the adage that the important thing in life isn't whether you win or lose that really counts, but how you play your game.

Other people can help you to achieve your goals of happiness. Find someone who can be your mentor in applying what you have learned in this book. If they also have a goal of their own, which is similar to one of yours, such as sticking to a diet, you can support one another. If you are married, your spouse might be the ideal person to fill the role. Or it could be anyone close enough to you that they have an interest in seeing you achieve your goal. Tell your mentor about your goals and daily objectives and have them agree to check up on you every once in a while to ensure that you comply with your program.

Finally, remember how important other people are to the general happiness of your life. Think back upon the times when you were really happy. The chances are that you were with other people at those moments, and that had a lot to do with your happiness. Data shows that people who are with others laugh five times as much as those who are alone. Among occupations, those who are directly helping others, such as social workers, teachers, mothers, nurses, and doctors, are among the happiest in our society.

Children are a special category. They're filled with optimism, energy, and enthusiasm. Catch it from them. You don't have to be a parent. Do you have younger cousins, nephews, or nieces? Do you have neighbors or friends who have children you could interact with? You could volunteer in a school, your religious community, boy or girl scouts, a sports team, hospital, church, or any other organization that helps children in their challenging path toward becoming adults.

I live right in the middle of New York City, and one of my favorite recreational activities on the weekend is to go for a walk in Central Park. For those of you not familiar with Central Park, it was created back in 1856 in a bold plan to provide a permanent area that would be all grass and trees where the residents of crowded New York City could go to find peace and quiet among the joys of nature. It consists of 843 acres and is a little over three miles long.

I love to go there simply to watch all the other people and all the activities they engage in. The park visitors are from every conceivable ethnic background and social level. They are engaged in dozens of activities from bicycle riding to row boating, to jogging, roller skating, playing baseball, dancing, Frisbee throwing, dining, people watching, and just relaxing.

The point is that all these people have come for a common purpose, to enjoy themselves in peace and harmony. And they usually succeed in both.

Chapter 13:
How Mental Health Professionals Can Help

Americans are spending more time seeking professional help for their mental welfare than ever before. The number of psychologists, psychiatrists, and mental health professionals is growing every year and has reached over 400,000. Are there really that many people who are neurotic? Or, is there something else going on? And more importantly, do all those hours and dollars being spent result in satisfactory outcomes for the clients? That's the million-dollar question that we'll be looking into.

It's my firm belief that most of the people who are seeing these therapists are totally mentally healthy. What they're really seeking isn't relief from any serious neurosis, such as a strong desire to commit suicide or illusions that they're a reincarnation of Joan of Arc, but rather people who are just having a difficult time being happy. It seems that as people get better educated and have more and more choices in the world, they may also become less and less happy. This could be because as our standard of living rises, our expectations of happiness also rise. Therefore, it's easier to believe that there must be something wrong with our lives when our standard of living goes up, but our level of happiness doesn't. We believe that we deserve more than we are getting.

So, we turn to professionals to find out what's wrong with us. Why aren't we having more fun in the world? Why are we too often bored with our lives? We go to therapists because we have questions like these. Then, after several months or years of seeking help, we have an additional question. After all the time and money we have spent on psychological therapy, has there been any measurable improvement in our life? And even if there was, we may wonder whether we would have improved without the therapy just from the natural maturation we have gone through in the intervening years.

There are many reasons for this ambiguity about seeing a therapist. One reason is that mental health is a much less well-defined topic than our normal questions about physical health.

If you have a pain in your leg, you know exactly what it is. You may know when it started, and you know how much it hurts. You also know that there must be a specific reason for the pain. So, you go to a doctor, and he makes his diagnosis.

You don't need to tell him what's wrong because after he takes an x-ray, he can clearly see the problem. He looks at the results and sees that, for some reason, your knee bones are rubbing against one another without the right amount of space between them.

He now knows exactly what treatment choices are available. Perhaps you will need a knee replacement, or maybe you only need some physical therapy. Or the doctor might say that these things come and go, and you should just take some over-the-counter pain killer. In any event, you either get specific advice, or the doctor undertakes some action, such as an operation. In either case, the doctor most likely has been able to solve your problem.

Seeing a therapist doesn't work that way. Because of the nature of the problems patients have, it can't work this way. You can't go to a therapist and say, "I want you to solve my problems, and I want you to make me happy." It doesn't work that way because everyone's problem is slightly different from anyone else's, and everyone's emotional background is unique.

You can go to a barber or beautician and say, "Cut my hair" or "Give me a new styling," and while the staff is doing that, you sit there reading one of your favorite magazines or having a conversation with someone. Then you look at yourself in the mirror and walk out feeling that you look at least 40% better than when you came in.

A successful treatment from a therapist is completely different because you can't be just passive as you are at your beautician or barber. Seeing a therapist requires your full and active participation, and that's a major difference from many other professional consultations. A good orthopedist may be able to set your broken wrist while you are watching television, but the greatest psychological therapist in the world can't cure you of anything if you aren't an active participant. To a very large degree, even when you see a therapist, you must cure yourself. The role of the therapist is to facilitate your improvement, but he can't do it for you.

The contrast with visits to the doctor starts at the first interaction that consists of your describing your problem. With the doctor, the complaint may be almost obvious. This is the opposite of the mental health patient, who may look completely normal. The person who goes to see a mental health professional must explain to the therapist what her problem is. Her complaint may be that she just doesn't seem to be finding the satisfaction in life that she expected, and she lists all the problems she has in her work, plus the problems she has with her relationships with men, perhaps some problems with her family, or some of her friends and even perhaps in her recreation activities. Nothing gives her the joy it used to. She doesn't want to get up in the morning, can't lose weight, has a boss who isn't supportive of her and often seems to be outright critical, etc. Where does the therapist begin?

Almost always, there are complaints about the other people in the patient's life. The boy or girlfriend who wants this and that but never has time to listen to the patient's problems; the parent nagging because the patient isn't married yet, or doesn't have children yet, or doesn't phone often enough; the friend who let him/her down by siding with someone else when a dispute arose, and so on. Some people go to a therapist asking what they can do to change their lives. But most of them go to complain about the injustices and incompetence they have had to endure at the hands of other people and to find out what they can do about it.

Marriage counselors see this all the time. A couple comes to them seeking advice on how they can make their marriage work better. But that isn't really what the couple is there for. The wife is actually there so she can tell someone all the hurtful things that her husband has done to her, and the husband is there so he can explain to someone that his wife isn't so easy to live with either, and he's getting tired of her trying to boss him around. Either spouse may even have brought a list of the other's imperfections to the session. And of course, each one believes to the bottom of their heart that they have been bending over backward to be the perfect spouse. It's a situation that can be very difficult to resolve.

Unlike our earlier medical problem where there was no question as to what the problem was, in this case, there isn't even any agreement on that. The wife is there because the husband's behavior is unbearable, and the husband is there because he can't stand the way his wife treats him. No one wants to change their own behavior, and each one thinks that the other must change his/her behavior. Not an easy situation for any therapist, no matter how talented they may be.

There are two basic challenges in mental therapy. As I've already mentioned, the first is that everything people do they do for a reason which is that they must get some benefit from what they do, even if that benefit is very short term and causes much larger problems for them in the future. Take any problem, and you can see that this is the case. For example, if a person is overweight, you might ask why they eat more than they should when they know that it isn't good for them. Even when they know that it's unhealthy, they're still overeating, which means there is some motivation or benefit that makes them want to do it.

What this benefit is can vary with each person, but often people eat too much because they're feeling insecure or unhappy. Eating is a natural function that produces a sense of satisfaction and wellbeing. So, it should come as no surprise that when some people are feeling down, they attempt to resolve that feeling by eating, and if it's a strong feeling, they may respond by overeating.

That person is acting based upon the short-term goal of feeling better now and is ignoring the much greater long-term costs of being overweight. The therapist's job, therefore, is to persuade the patient that they'll have a far happier life if they stop overeating. This may not be easy to do because breaking long-term habits can often cause stress and discomfort.

A very similar sequence of events occurs with people who are relying on alcohol to get them over their problems. They're feeling apprehensive about something and believe that a drink will help them overcome those feelings. If one drink doesn't do the trick, then they have another one, and so on. They know full well that by getting drunk, they can be ruining their reputations and destroying their life as well.

If the therapist does understand what the patient is getting out of the self-destructive behavior, then it's their job to point this out to the patient. But beyond this, what can the therapist do? The short-term goal may be so powerful in some people that they're simply unable to give up this self-destructive behavior.

This leads to the second difficulty of therapy, which is that in the end, the therapist can't cure the problem. It's the patients themselves who must bring about the cure, and this is often difficult. Unlike the doctor at the beginning of this chapter who was able to recommend a diagnosis that would cure the problem, the therapist can't replace a bad habit. He can only point out the long-term negatives that the patient is creating in exchange for an almost worthless short-term benefit and urge the patient to change their lifestyle. But it's the patient who must do the changing.

However, we must not overlook the many benefits that patients of therapists receive. Why else would so many people spend so much time and money on going to them? Many people have been seeing their therapists for years, so there have to be solid reasons.

First, it can be very comforting to talk with someone who is really interested in you, and not themselves, and is willing to talk about you and about you only for an extended period of time. If you think about it, how many conversations have you had recently with your friends where the entire conversation was about you?

And if it only was just about you, then how long was it before your friend decided that you had spent enough time on you and brought up another subject. Such a conversation focused on you would probably occur only when there had been a major event in your life that would only occur infrequently, certainly not every week. The importance of talking with another person who really cares about you can't be overstated. Even if the other person only cares enough to ask the right questions and to remember what was said in previous sessions.

Second, psychological therapy has been called "paid friendship," but that's not the worst thing in the world. It means that there is always someone you can go to who knows your problems, knows how you are trying to solve them, and is willing to discuss this with you in a professional, impartial manner. Of course, you could always discuss your problems with your friends, but they may not want to criticize you for fear of upsetting you and perhaps detracting from your friendship. Besides, they are also participants in your society and therefore may have viewpoints that are similar to yours and will therefore not influence you to change.

If you are a mother who is having a problem with an adult child, the chances are very good that you are going to want to discuss it with a friend who is also the mother of an adult child. Why not? She might have had the same problem as you and at least can identify with the situation. So, she gives you her opinion, but no matter how hard she tries to be objective, it's still the opinion of another mother of an adult child.

It could be that neither of you can really understand the viewpoint of the child, which is very likely quite different from the mothers' perspective. At least, a therapist has the benefit that he/she may not be the mother of an adult child, and therefore, may have a more objective understanding of the child's point of view. This type of understanding can be of particular benefit to the patient if the problem under discussion involves a male/female relationship and the therapist is the opposite sex from the patient.

The second benefit of seeing a therapist is that, in most cases, they may have a wide range of experience in working with situations like yours. Each one of us is unique, and no two problems are exactly alike; however, difficulties can be broken down into classifications, and it's probable that an experienced therapist has had patients with a problem similar to yours and has learned an effective way of improving the situation.

For example, every adult is quite different when it comes to deciding what they should do in the future, but an experienced therapist could know what questions will bring out the real needs and desires of the person who has come to him for assistance in making that decision. One patient may be struggling with whether he should go into the Air Force or go to work for a corporation, and another patient can't decide whether to work for a major foundation or become a yoga instructor, but the thought patterns that go into making that determination may be very similar.

If you are already seeing a therapist, one thing you should keep in mind is that the longer you have been seeing them, the less likely it is that you will be able to make a real change in your life. That explains why some people have been seeing therapists for years. Clearly, if they really have a problem, the combination of that therapist with that patient has not been able to solve their problem.

If you are one of those people who is continuing to see your therapist for the reasons given above and you realize that it's really a paid friendship or a chance for you to get sympathy and validation, then recognize it for what it is. Just don't kid yourself into thinking that you are likely to have a breakthrough that will turn you into a fully self-fulfilled person.

As the author and psychotherapist Jonathan Alpert has noted, people who have more than twenty sessions of therapy are likely to wind up in a dead-end relationship. You can discern his point of view from the title of his book, which is "Be Fearless: Change Your Life in 28 Days." He has two themes:

1. Most people go to therapists with specific problems such as unfulfilling jobs or relationships and are fearful of change that leads to anxiety and depression, and

2. That what these patients need is a therapist who is active and engaging, rather than one who is cautious and non-intrusive and whose main role is to listen.

If you are in a long-term therapy that isn't going anywhere, you can take a leave from your therapy for a month or two and see what the results are. The positive results will be that you are saving what may be a substantial amount of money and freeing up the time that you spend with the therapist. You also might find that your life isn't any worse off by not having someone listen to you once a week.

If, at the end of a month or two, you find that you miss the sessions, you have a choice of going back to your former therapist or looking for a new one who has a different approach. Incidentally, you might find that your therapist is unlikely to be the one to suggest that the therapy has come to a close.

Another positive reason for seeing a professional is that if they think it's appropriate, they can write you a prescription for anti-depression medication(s) that work to make most patients happier than they were before. If the professional can't write you a prescription themselves, they can recommend you to someone who can. The best advisors for antidepressants are pharmacologists who are M.D.s specializing in drug treatments and consultations.

This may sound like a minor miracle, but it's true. These drugs work by rebalancing some of the natural chemicals in our brains. Unfortunately, they are not guaranteed to work, and they are ineffective for some patients. There are many different ones, such as Prozac, Celexa, escitalopram, and Zoloft. They may have some minor side effects, and once you start taking them, you should continue taking them indefinitely because if you stop and become despondent, you could become more depressed than you were before you started taking them. However, I highly recommend that if after reading this book and following its suggestions, you still don't feel as happy as you think you should be, that you consult a mental health professional to learn if you could benefit from them

Because of the many disappointments in my own life, which I mentioned in the early part of this book, I myself started taking antidepressants a few years ago and have been very pleased with the results. I also know many other people whose lives have been literally transformed by them. If you feel the need for more help in your march toward a more joyful life, do give them a try.

Closing Thoughts

We've come to the end of our journey, and we've covered a lot of territory. It might be worthwhile to have a quick review of some of the important lessons we've learned in this book.

The first lesson that underlies this entire book is the Three Great Rules of Happiness, which are:

1. Want What You Have.

This is another way of saying that instead of always wanting more, you should be happy with what you have, including the love of your friends and family, your health, and the opportunity to remake yourself into a happier person.

2. Do What You Can.

While this may seem simplistic at first, it's actually a demanding two-part principle that requires you to think of what you are able to do and then urges you to do it. It's a realistic counterpoint to the absurd phrase, "What man can conceive, man can achieve."

3. Be the Best You Are.

This is a practical and moral guideline that doesn't require you to reach out and be a better person than you ever were. It only asks you to use the highest level of your mind, which is already there. You don't need to climb to new moral heights or capabilities because your brain already knows what it's capable of. You just need to give it direction and motivation.

The remainder of the book was devoted to the practical implementation of these rules by using examples of actual situations. First, we learned the difference between pleasure and true happiness; then, we learned the many ways to climb out of bad moods. Next, we learned about excessive pre-conditions that can needlessly restrict our choices and about dangerous behavior patterns that can ruin our lives. We then found out why our lives needed to have a serious component. Finally, we learned how mental health professionals can help us.

If you want a quick reminder of what this book was all about, just remember the Three Great Rules of Happiness. If you want an even quicker reminder of how to become happy, you can look to the Bible verses (Luke 6:31 & Matthew 7:12), which says:

> "**Do onto others**, as you would have them do unto you."

Yes, you've heard this before, but it's still solid advice; two thousand years later.

Postlude

Max Ansbacher provides personal happiness counseling in Manhattan, New York City and Palm Beach, Florida, and everywhere else via Zoom. His email is:

aimmaxwork@gmail.com

THE
END

Made in United States
Orlando, FL
07 November 2024

53574532R00124